W9-BWN-788

Secrets
for Secondary
School
Teachers

To
Savta
and
Pop Pop

Secrets
for Secondary
School
Teachers

How to Succeed
in Your First Year

Ellen Kottler, Jeffrey A. Kottler, Cary J. Kottler

CORWIN PRESS, INC.
A Sage Publications Company
Thousand Oaks, California

For information:

Corwin Press, Inc.
A Sage Publications Company
2455 Teller Road
Thousand Oaks, California 91320
E-mail: order@corwinpress.com

SAGE Publications Ltd.
6 Bonhill Street
London EC2A 4PU
United Kingdom

SAGE Publications India Pvt. Ltd.
M-32 Market
Greater Kailash I
New Delhi 110 048 India

Printed in the United States of America

Library of Congress Cataloging-in-Publication Data

Kottler, Ellen.
  Secrets for secondary school teachers: How to succeed in your
first year / by Ellen Kottler, Jeffrey A. Kottler, and Cary J.
Kottler.
    p. cm.
  ISBN 0-8039-6603-2 (cloth : acid-free paper). — ISBN
0-8039-6604-0 (pbk. : acid-free paper)
  1. First year teachers. 2. High school teachers. 3. Teacher
orientation. I. Kottler, Jeffrey A. II. Kottler, Cary J.
III. Title.
LB2844.1.N4K67 1998
373.13—dc21   97-45326

99 00 01 02 03 10 9 8 7 6 5 4 3 2

Production Editor: Sanford Robinson
Production Assistant: Denise Santoyo
Typesetter: Danielle Dillahunt
Interior Designer: Rebecca Evans
Cover Designer: Marcia M. Rosenburg

Contents

CORWIN
PRESS

The Corwin Press logo—a raven striding across an open book—represents the happy union of courage and learning. We are a professional-level publisher of books and journals for K-12 educators, and we are committed to creating and providing resources that embody these qualities. Corwin's motto is "Success for All Learners."

Preface

Excitement. Curiosity. Apprehension. No, make that terror! These are just a few of the reactions that new teachers have as they anticipate their first year in the classroom.

The book work is done. The closely supervised practica and field experiences are over. No more taking tests or writing papers—now, you are the one who gets to grade them!

You now have the freedom to organize your own life, away from the confines of the university. Finally, you will start earning money doing something you hope you will truly love. Impressionable minds to mold in positive directions. It will be so great, you think, creating the kind of classroom that you always wanted as a student—a place where real learning takes place, where kids have fun, where there is order and support, where differences are honored, and yet everyone works together as a team.

Certainly, you have seen enough from your classroom observations and field experiences to know that there is tremendous diversity in the ways that teachers organize their classrooms and their lives. You have seen chaos in action—teachers who are jokes in their schools, who earn little respect from their colleagues and even less from their students. You have observed other teachers throughout your life who are truly masters at their craft, absolutely brilliant in their abilities to win friends and influence people. A few of these individuals may even be responsible for your own decision to be a teacher.

Now you stand poised, ready to begin your own career as an educator. You don't want to be one of those teachers who is eaten alive, who burns out after a few years, or even worse—who keeps teaching year after year, long after the point where he or she cares any longer about children and their learning. Neither do you want to be the kind of teacher who is average, who puts in the years, accumulates time in the retirement system, processes children like an assembly line, doing an adequate but undistinguished job. No, you want to be a *great* teacher.

Your dream can very well become a reality . . . if you make some sound decisions from the beginning. This means applying what you learned in your teacher education program in such a way that it is consistent with the realities of your particular school. It means catching on rather quickly to the innumerable traps and challenges you will face during your first year as a teacher. It means recruiting the right mentors who can support you along the way.

This book is intended to serve as one of your mentors, a handbook that you can consult periodically to prepare yourself for any of the usual challenges you are likely to face. It has been written by a teacher-administrator, a teacher-counselor-educator, and a high school student specifically to reflect the realities of what most likely leads to success for beginning teachers.

We have brought together the most practical elements from your course work, from the education literature, and advice from master teachers to provide you with guidance during your first professional teaching position. The book includes tips and secrets that experienced teachers have developed to simplify, organize, and reduce the stress associated with the first year on the job. Many of the tips are illustrated with vignettes that show how they can be applied in action.

A series of brief, focused chapters addresses a number of topics that are absolutely critical for teachers. Beginning with the basics of orienting yourself to your school and classroom, we then provide specific and practical advice for not only surviving but flourishing during your first year of teaching. These issues include such things as getting to know students, parents, and community; captivating and holding student attention; organizing your room and learning your way around the school; dealing with sources of stress, such as being evaluated and grading others; figuring out the culture of the school so you can make a place for yourself; and preparing yourself for all the things you needed to learn in school but somehow missed along the way. We cover pragmatic realities related to problem students and colleagues, handling paperwork, networking with others for support, preparing for a substitute, dealing with disappointments and unrealistic expectations, as well as maintaining your enthusiasm and planning for your own future.

The purpose of this book is to provide teacher education students, beginning teachers, and those returning to the field after an extended absence with the practical information they need to be successful in the classroom. The topics we selected are those that are of immediate concern to beginners in the field.

In addition to its use by teachers during their first few years of practice, this book can also be used as a primary or secondary text in practica, internships, and student teaching experiences. Usually, texts are not ordered for these courses because of the emphasis on experience; however, this guide fills a needed gap in students' bases of knowledge by providing them with practical strategies that will help them to survive and flourish in their first years in their new profession.

About the Authors

Ellen Kottler received her bachelor's degree from the University of Michigan, her master's degree from Eastern Michigan University, and her Ed.S. from the University of Nevada, Las Vegas. She has been a secondary teacher for over 20 years, in public, private, and alternative schools at the secondary level, teaching a range of courses in social studies, humanities, and foreign language. She is currently an administrative specialist for the Department of Curriculum and Professional Development in the Clark County School District in Las Vegas.

She is the author of *Children with Limited English: Teaching Strategies for the Regular Classroom* (1994) and coauthor of *Teacher as Counselor* (1993).

Jeffrey A. Kottler is Professor of Counseling and Educational Psychology at Texas Tech University. He is the author or coauthor of over 30 books in education and psychology, including *On Being A Teacher* (1993), *Beyond Blame: A New Way of Resolving Conflicts in Relationships* (1994), *Classrooms Under the Influence* (1995), *Success With Challenging Students* (1997), and *What's Really Said in the Teachers' Lounge* (1997).

Cary J. Kottler has attended public school in the United States and New Zealand. He is currently a student at Green Valley High School in Henderson (Las Vegas), Nevada, where he attends class and plays baseball.

xii

Learning Your Way Around the School

1

"Visitors please report to the Principal's Office," reads the sign at the entrance to the school. Indeed, you are a visitor that first year, with all the appropriate levels of confusion and disorientation that are typical for an intrepid explorer who is operating in unknown territory without a map.

As many times as you have visited a school previously, during field placements or perhaps even as a parent or relative of a student, you are always struck by how big the place seems. Everyone seems to know just where they are going, always in a hurry, making contact with as many people as they can, rushing to the next class before the bell rings. The place is a maze of offices, rooms, hallways, labs, each connected by a layout that probably once made sense to someone in charge of designing things. To the newcomer, however, whether an entering student or first-year teacher, the school seems hopelessly inhospitable.

Orient Yourself

Your first job is to learn your way around. We don't mean just memorizing the quickest route from the entrance to your assigned classroom; rather, we mean orienting yourself completely to every nook and cranny in the building. After you've gotten the official tour from the principal and department head, make it a priority to get "unofficial" guides from an experienced teacher, a secretary, a student, and a custodian. This is the place you will be spending most of your life during the coming years, so you will want to orient yourself as quickly and comprehensively as you can.

An experienced staff member recalls,

> I remember one new teacher who never left her classroom during the day except to go to the bathroom down the hall. At first, we thought she was just snooty or unsociable. Only later, we learned she was so afraid of getting lost that she thought it best to just remain in one spot as long as she could.

Make Friends With
the School Secretaries

Most people think that principals hold the power in schools. Well, they are certainly the designated authority figures, and they certainly wield their share of power over what happens in the school. But the people who control access to the administration, the ones who are the best connected to all facets of the school's operation, those who know the most efficient ways to get things done, as well as the most important gossip, are the school secretaries.

In learning your way around the school, the school secretary will be your first point of contact. She or he will help you get settled, introduce you around, and help you process the appropriate paperwork. Even if the principal does this himself or herself, you would be well-advised to spend some time getting to know the secretaries later. Ultimately, they can be your strongest supporters or worst obstacles throughout your career.

You will probably have a few thousand questions to address to your first school guide. Rather than overwhelming the person with the sheer number of inquiries, prioritize the most critical ones, and save the rest to ask others later. In fact, unless you are a complete pest, asking questions can be a great way to meet as many different staff members as possible.

Rules and Regulations

The principal or secretary is likely to give you a map of the school as well as the official Teacher's Handbook that tells you about the rules, regulations, and expectations for your job. Read the manual carefully when you get the chance, but keep in mind that these are only the publicly espoused values, not necessarily those that are most dominant in the school culture. To find out the "underground" version of the rules and regulations, you will need to interview quite a number of students and staff members over time. This is how you will find out what is really expected of you.

You will want to discover

- Who has the most power and control in the school?
- Who and what influences the principal the most?
- How do decisions get made?
- What are the major conflicts that erupt most consistently?
- What coalitions have formed among staff members, and on what basis do these groups maintain their membership?

These are just a few questions to consider. More will be suggested later. Initially, however, you will want to orient yourself with the handbook and the physical layout of the building. At this point, your department head should also be helpful with your schedule, texts, and other assignments.

Building Orientation

Once you have been escorted to your assigned classroom and left to your own devices, allow yourself sufficient time to revel in the feelings that you are experiencing. This classroom is *your* room: the place where you will be working your magic. There are bulletin boards to dress up, furniture to rearrange according to your liking, supplies to order and put away. Mostly, though, you just want to get a feel for the space, personalize it, make it yours, at least to the point where it starts to feel a little familiar.

Once you have gotten settled, there are a number of other important places that you will want to locate from your room. These include

- Principal's office
- Deans' office
- Counselors' office
- Attendance office
- Registrar's office
- Nurse's office
- Teacher's lounge
- Library
- Cafeteria
- School banker
- Graphic arts and copy room
- Student restroom facilities

Safety Concerns

As part of your school orientation, you will also need to familiarize yourself with safety procedures in the event of some emergency: fires for certain, and depending on your location, hurricanes, tornadoes, earthquakes, or volcanic eruptions. (According to a posted sign in a New Zealand school, in the event of such an eruption, you should close all windows and doors).

In learning your way around the school, make sure to find out where the fire alarm nearest your room is located, where to direct students in the event of fire drills, and where the designated shelters are for other disasters.

School Traditions

Every school has its own unique culture and customs, some of them established by the administration, such as school mascots and cheers, others emerging from student or staff input. Homecoming celebrations, school dances, and other events have many customs associated with them. These traditions are as much a part of the school experience as anything to do with the physical building, and you would be well-advised to familiarize yourself with these customs.

I (Ellen) recall beginning a new job in a high school that had more than its share of school spirit. Typical of schools in small Southern towns, much of the conversation during my first day was about upcoming football games that the Razorbacks would be playing. I listened intently to the discussion, trying to pick out clues as to what was going on, but I was lost. I had no idea what a Razorback even was. People were aghast at my ignorance and then dutifully explained that it was a kind of hedgehog, another creature that I had no direct experience with.

The reactions of my colleagues got my attention so that I knew I had to devote considerable attention not only to the history of the Razorbacks but to other school traditions. In similar fashion, you will want to research how your school got its name, who its primary benefactors are, and landmark incidents in its history.

Lunch Options

Part of your initial orientation should include exploring options for lunch. There is tremendous diversity in how teachers spend their break time. Some prefer the solitude to relax or go for a walk. Others catch up on grading exams while they nibble a sandwich. For beginning teachers, we are unequivocal: You *must* use this time constructively to make important contacts, network with other staff members, and integrate yourself into the school culture.

In your first weeks on the job, you will want to experiment with different lunch venues: the school cafeteria, the teachers' lounge, and if there's time, joining different groups as they go out for a quick meal. It is not the food that is the issue but rather the opportunities to meet as many other staff members as you can. In most schools, this is where the important decisions get made. Because the subject is so important, we will discuss it in greater detail in Chapter 8.

Meeting Others

Learning your way around the school most often involves meeting other teachers and staff members. This is where you find out what has worked before and what is usually not successful. This is how you get your endless questions answered. It is also where you will find the support you need to deal with the inevitable challenges you will face.

When you talk to others, remind them of your name. Frequently, there are many new faces and names (especially after the students report to school), so it is very helpful if you mention your name *and* what you teach to facilitate the "getting to know you" process.

One secret to help learn the names of the staff people is to get a copy of the previous year's yearbook and study it intently. Some hair styles may have changed and some pictures will be outdated, but the annual can be an excellent reference. In fact, there is none better to help you get a handle on the official goings-on of the school, the performances of the athletic teams, and the school traditions that are maintained.

Take a Breath

The first year of teaching is indeed one of the most exhilarating and challenging experiences that you will ever have. You will be tested in ways that you can't imagine. You will learn some things about the world, about the process of learning, that will surprise you. Most of all, you will learn a lot about yourself, some of which may frighten you, whereas some will delight you.

There will be precious little time for contemplation or planning. Your time will be eaten up in meetings, extracurricular activities, and just trying to stay ahead of the students. Many of the things you had hoped to do will be put aside, at least temporarily. That's okay. Your main job is just to learn your way around, to experiment with styles and methods until you find things that work best for you.

Be patient with yourself. Your principal and other colleagues know well what kind of stress you are under. They will mostly be understanding of the mistakes you make. Those who are harsh critics (and there will be some) often act insensitively because they treat everyone that way; it may not be personal.

It takes time, but eventually you will learn your way around. Those who don't believe that are fooling themselves. Remember well what you are going through; before you know it, you will be the expert showing someone else around.

2 Organizing Your Room

Once you can find your way around the school, the next priority is to organize the personal space in which you will be operating. You learned in education classes that the classroom environment is critical in setting the tone for everything else that you do. You know from your own experiences as a student that there exists a quite different atmosphere in a room that is drab versus one that positively vibrates with energy. You know that quite different things happen in a room that is organized with desks in neat rows versus those arranged in a semicircle.

Depending on the culture of your school, what other teachers are doing around you, what subjects you are teaching, and what your personal philosophy of learning is, you will want to give considerable attention to organizing your room so that you will accomplish your desired goals. Consider not only your needs but also those of students.

I (Jeffrey) once shared a classroom with another teacher who had a very different style than my own. The first thing I'd do each day was rearrange the room with all the desks in a big circle so that students could see and talk to one another. I wanted a more democratic structure than a traditional teacher-centered classroom, one that encouraged interaction. Because this was a class in social skills training, this particular physical environment was entirely appropriate.

My colleague, however, was teaching a content-oriented course in a far more traditional manner. He was threatened by the things I was doing in my class that directly contradicted many of the values he considered most important: discipline, control, and authority. He believed learning took place through his lectures, whereas I valued student interaction. Our room arrangements reflected these pedagogical styles.

Because I was a new teacher and because my colleague had a lot of power in the school, he worked behind the scenes to make me comply to his standards. The principal approached me apologetically that he had some complaints because I was leaving my room "in disarray" for the next class. Perhaps it would be better, he admonished me, if I just left the desks "the way they were supposed to be." I was appalled, of course, but I learned a valuable lesson about how our own actions as teachers affect, and even sometimes threaten, other colleagues. In the future, I shared my plans for seating arrangements with my principal and got him "on my side" in advance. I also required the students to return the chairs to their traditional placement before leaving the room.

We mention this object lesson not to discourage you from taking risks, experimenting with alternative classroom structures, or expressing your unique style through your teaching—quite the contrary. We hope you do create a classroom environment that is radical enough to keep students' interest and encourages them to think for themselves and challenge ideas. Just remember: Everything you do as a new teacher is being watched by others and evaluated according to their standards.

Inventory Resources

The first step in organizing your room is to check out the resources you have to work with. Spend a few minutes sitting in different parts of the room to observe what it feels like. Imagine you are a student sitting there, daydreaming about something far more important than whatever is going on in the room at the time. Note what is within the visual field from each point in the room. Listen for the acoustics as well, to hear how sound travels, both for sounds within the classroom and potentially distracting noises outside.

Survey where the bulletin boards are located as well as the chalkboards, the pencil sharpeners, the lights, the electric sockets, the overhead projector, the computer, or any other available equipment. Remember, when you use any audiovisual aids, you will need access to electricity and ways to avoid glare so the screens are clearly visible. If you have a telephone line in your room, you will want a desk and chair nearby. Also note what type of heating or air conditioning system is used. Will students be subject to strong air blowing on them, depending on where they sit?

Next, look at the furniture and equipment that has been assigned to your room. Do you have bookshelves, tables, chairs, desks, file cabinet, wardrobe, a computer? Is there any audio-visual equipment in the room? What items do you feel are most important to you? Start making a list of what is missing. Keep in mind that the resources available in your school may not match with what you were once told in teacher training was mandatory for good learning to take place. Technical aids are useful, but they are not imperative for good learning to occur. For now, make a list of what you need, and hold onto it until you figure out the most politically expedient ways to lobby for what you want.

Most schools have an audiovisual center where the equipment is kept. Even if you don't have permanent equipment, you might be able to gain access to things on an as-needed basis. For example, most foreign language teachers have a television monitor, a VCR, and cassette recorders reserved for them, purchased with federal grant money. Can arrangements be made for you to keep equipment in your room on a regular basis? Some schools even have opaque projectors available for your use. And don't forget the possibilities of record players. Many schools have wonderful 33⅓ recordings of music, speeches, poems, and plays to enhance classroom experiences. In addition, many districts have media centers with wide varieties of instructional materials available for teachers to reserve and use. In some states, the resources are kept at regional rather than district levels.

Flow and Movement

Room arrangements are critical to maintain student safety as well as engagement with class activities. From what direction will the students enter the room? Will they have sufficient space to walk by with their big book bags?

You have probably already given consideration to how you want to arrange the room to fit your teaching style and course content. Will students be listening most of the time or working with partners? How much will cooperative group work be a part of your classes? Will students be interacting a lot with one another?

Specific seating arrangements are designed to accomplish different goals. As you walk around the school visiting other teachers, check out the ways they have arranged their rooms. Note the advantages and disadvantages of each. Some of the more common configurations include these:

- Traditional rows of desks to maximize the number of students in the room and maintain order
- Rows of desks facing each other across a center divide to encourage student-teacher interaction
- Horseshoe arrangement with desks facing the front
- Tables seating small groups of 4 to 6 students
- Desks in one large circle to facilitate interaction
- A "fishbowl" design, with an inner and outer circle of desks

Of course, a combination of arrangements may be possible, depending on the particular learning activity. In fact, one way to keep students engaged is to devise ways that move them around from one seating arrangement to another. Nevertheless, you will still wish to settle on a relatively stable arrangement to begin with, at least to facilitate taking attendance until you get to know the students.

One other consideration in space design is related to managing student behavior. Because issues related to classroom behavior and discipline will be among your greatest challenges, you will want to make sure to arrange things in such a way that allows you full view of everything going on in the room. Also, you will want to consider potential problems that could emerge. For example, some students will find countless pieces of paper or Kleenex to throw away. Their pencil leads will always be breaking. If you don't want students to cross your line of vision during your instruction, place the objects they need access to, such as boxes of tissue, paper, pencil sharpeners, and waste baskets, at strategic points around, or on either side of, the room.

Space Design

There is no sense whining and complaining about what you don't have in the way of resources, equipment, and furniture; for now, make the best of what you do have.

One place to start is with display space in the form of bulletin boards and even blank walls. Because you can figure that at about any given moment of time, more that half your students are in the midst of fantasy or otherwise occupied with thoughts about their families, friends, love lives, or lack thereof, it is important that you design displays in ways that are visually stimulating but not distracting.

With me (Cary) or most of my friends, we could care less about stuff like bulletin boards. I can't figure out what teachers think is so important about them. Who cares?

But my math teacher did something that was kinda cool. He put, on one of the side boards, a sheet of paper with the year, 1997, lettered on top. Then he had numbers going down the side from 1 to 100. Whenever you were bored or in the mood to do so, you could go up to the bulletin board and invent an equation using the numbers 1, 9, 9, and 7 whose answer would be a number from 1 to 100. For example, $1 + 9 + 9 + 7 = 26$; $1 + (9 \times 9) + 7 = 89$. The challenge was fun.

In spite of this skepticism, bulletin boards are useful for brightening up the room as well as helping you to emphasize key points of given lessons. They allow you to post general information about school activities as well as current events related to your content area. Keep in mind that spaces in the back of the room should be designed for purposes different than those to the sides or the front if the students face the front, such as motivational or decorative, because the students see them only as they enter.

You might want to hang pictures, photos, or posters to create a homey feel to the room. It all depends on what mood and images you want to communicate to your students. In a history class, you would expect to see pictures of past achievements. In an English class, you might see rules to use for writing, or programs for plays, or pictures of famous authors. In a math class, you might see applications of formulas, geometric patterns, or famous mathematicians. But these are only traditional applications; you can be a lot more creative than that!

In deciding what to do with your bulletin boards, consider the following functions that are possible:

- Informative—Giving facts
- Rule giving—Guidelines to follow
- Demonstrative—Showing examples
- Motivational—Giving inspiration
- Stimulating—Posing a question or new idea
- Rewarding—Displaying student work
- Aesthetic—A reflection of your own interests and likes
- Reinforcing—Giving support
- Entertaining—Using humor

Equipment Checklist

Before you put your plan into action and start moving heavy furniture around the room, first design a blueprint on a piece of paper, positioning each piece of furniture and equipment. Consult the following checklists for items you might wish to consider in your plan:

Permanent Features

___ Placement of door   ___ Location of windows

___ Electric sockets   ___ Chalk or dry-erase boards

___ Bulletin boards   ___ Lighting

___ Light switch   ___ Telephone line

___ Pencil sharpeners   ___ Immovable cabinets

Technical Equipment

___ Computer(s)   ___ Television

___ VCR   ___ Laser disc player

___ Audio tape player   ___ Overhead projector

___ Record player   ___ Opaque projector

Furniture

___ Teacher's desk and chair   ___ File cabinet(s)

___ Wardrobe(s)   ___ Table(s)

___ Student desks or tables   ___ Chairs

___ Waste basket(s)   ___ Bookshelves

Supplies Checklist

Once the furniture is arranged, you will next need to concentrate on supplies that will be useful in your work. First, take inventory of what is already available in your room. Then, make a list of items you will need based on these suggestions:

___ Lined paper	___ Plain paper
___ Construction paper	___ Paper punch
___ Scotch tape	___ Masking tape
___ Book covers	___ File cards
___ Stapler	___ Staples
___ Paper clips	___ Post-it notes
___ Pens	___ Pencils
___ Rulers	___ Scissors
___ Computer disks	___ Video tapes
___ Hanging folders	___ File folders
___ Overhead markers	___ Dry-erase markers or chalk
___ Attendance book	___ Lesson plan book
___ Scantrons (machine-scorable answer sheets)	___ Snacks to munch on

In addition to these general supplies, you will also need those related to your subject—chemicals for science teachers, balls for physical education, paint for art. Consult with your department head and other colleagues for suggestions in this area.

Other Considerations

It is helpful to have a place in your room where students can find their makeup work due to an absence or pick up a paper that was passed back when they were absent. Some methods that teachers have used successfully are these:

- A notebook binder where handouts—instructional as well as homework—can be found for each given day
- A file folder, posted on the wall or in a drawer or in a box
- A calendar posted with each assignment listed
- A list of assignments on a poster board
- An area of the chalk board with the day or week's objectives and assignments

You will also want easy access to first aid supplies. Band-Aids are most commonly requested, but you will probably receive a disinfectant, cotton swabs, sterile gauze pads, and gloves as well in a first aid kit from the nurse's office. It is a good idea to include safety pins in the kit for torn clothing. For serious problems, you will refer the student to the school nurse or health aide. You will want to have the basic supplies immediately available so as not to waste class time looking for them.

Knowing Your Students 3

Now that we've got your room out of the way, it's time to concentrate on the students you will soon be meeting. Within a very short period of time, you will be exposed to over a hundred students, each with individual needs and unique names to memorize and pronounce correctly. If you think that's overwhelming, just think about foreign language teachers who not only have to learn the real names of each student but also their assigned Spanish or French or German (or Russian or Japanese or Latin) names.

Learning the names of students quickly is only one of your initial tasks; you will also want to accumulate some basic data on each of your students.

Collecting Information

One straightforward way to collect information on your students is to ask them to fill out index cards on the first day of class, beginning with their names on the top. You can also ask them to suggest ways to help you remember how to pronounce their names correctly.

Not all students go by their given names. Many have preferred nicknames. Some are diminutives such as "Jimmy" or "Susie." Others are common, such as "Junior" or "Bud." One boy told me (Ellen) he wanted to be called "Boogie." I wasn't sure what to make of that and I didn't want to embarrass myself. Because he wrote he was a football player, I went to see one of the coaches. I told him I had a student who wanted to be called "Boogie" and asked him what the story was. He assured me that it was okay; everyone called him Boogie.

On succeeding lines of the index card, there is room for all sorts of information. One line at a time can provide a place for the following: address, telephone number(s) [sometimes students have their own telephone lines], birthday, age, mother's or guardian's name and telephone numbers at home and work, and father's or guardian's name and telephone numbers at home and work. You may also want to inquire as to what hours the parents or guardians work.

Next, you might ask the students to answer questions related to language skills (e.g., What is your first language? What languages are spoken in the home? What languages do you read?). Here, you will learn if there is support in the home for English language (or foreign language) activities. Some students will not be able to get help with their homework if their parents do not speak English.

It is interesting to gather information about their interests and activities (e.g., Do you play an instrument? Do you play sports? What activities do you participate in before school? After school? How long?). Here, you will learn what responsibilities your students have—who babysits, who cooks for the family when parents are at work. It's also important to know whether the student works or not and if so, how many hours per week.

I (Ellen) had one student who was always falling asleep in class, although he seemed like a very capable learner. At first, I thought it was a motivational problem, then that he was just being obstructive. Finally, I remembered to look at his card, and I discovered an obvious clue: He was working 40 hours a week in a restaurant. No wonder he couldn't stay awake in class!

One last question that will give students a chance to give you information secretly is to ask, Is there anything you would like me as a teacher to know about you? This is particularly useful for gaining personal information. Students will write about things that they are not particularly comfortable telling you face to face. Problems are revealed: "I stutter." "I can't see from the back of the room." "I am really nervous about learning to drive." "My mom just had a new baby and the baby cries all night, so I don't get very much sleep."

You can personalize the questions to fit your subject area as well. In language classes, you might be interested in knowing if the students have pets or how many brothers and sisters they have, because these can be topics for future discussion in basic vocabulary. In English, you might ask, What is the last book you read or the best book you've read? In history class, you can ask what the last movie or best movie was that they've seen that related to a historical period. In math, you might ask, What would you like to review from last year?

The specific questions you ask are less important than collecting basic information about your students that will help you to get to know them. The cards provide an opportunity for your class members to tell you some things about themselves in a private, nonthreatening manner.

SAMPLE INFORMATION CARD

Cary Jay Kottler   Call me Cary.   Spanish name: Carlito
Born: Nov. 25, 1980   I'm 16.

We speak English at home, although my first language was
    Spanish when I lived in Peru when I was 2.
My mom works at the school district so I can't get in trouble.
    My dad works at the university.
Baseball is the most important thing to me. We've won 5 State
    Championships in a row.
If I can't play baseball professionally, then I have no clue what
    I'm going to do.
Besides baseball, I guess I like music, movies, and girls.
    Once in a while, I will read a book.
I gotta tell you: I'm not crazy about Spanish. Hopefully, you
    will change that for me.

Although the information cards can contain a lot of useful information, remember that you must ask students to write legibly.

One time, I (Ellen) misread a boy's first name and called a girl's name with his last name. Both of us were quite embarrassed. Sometimes, attendance lists are not provided until the second week of school, so your cards may be the only accurate information you have about who is in your class.

In the beginning of the school year, the cards can be organized alphabetically, for taking attendance and for record keeping. Later, they can be organized by calendar sequence so you can acknowledge birth dates. Being wished a "Happy Birthday" does much for a student's esteem.

The back of the cards can be used to keep records of parent contacts. There will be space for each date and time and notes about the nature of the conversation.

Special Events

Alerting yourself to special events in the lives of students will help you communicate your sincere interest as well as encourage them in areas that are most important to them. If you know from the information you gathered that a child is involved in forensics, band or orchestra, cheerleading, track, or the school newspaper, you can keep an eye out for times when you can let him or her know that you are following his or her progress.

When I (Cary) was in junior high school, one of my teachers made a point of congratulating me for having my bar mitzvah. This made a big impression on me. It let me know she really cared about me.

My favorite teachers have always been those who showed me that they really cared about me. Like when I pitch in a baseball game, a teacher will let me know that she knew about it. Even if I don't really like the class much, I will still give that teacher a break in ways I never would with someone who just acted like I wasn't important to her at all.

When I have a problem or something, the teacher I'm going to talk to is going to be the one who seems to care.

Paying attention to rites of passage and giving appropriate recognition will help cement relationships. For freshmen and sophomores, those special moments include getting braces off their teeth and getting their driver's licenses (refer back to the index cards to watch for upcoming birthdays). Most teens get their licenses on the first try, but some do not and may be disappointed. Some are not permitted to get their licenses right away (for example, their parents may feel they do not have enough driving experience, or they may be punishing them for some prior activity), and that can be a source of embarrassment. The first homecoming dance can be a time of great apprehension for boys and girls.

The big events for juniors are the college entrance exams. Results of test scores can be a confidence booster or a major letdown. For seniors, in the fall, early responses to college applications arrive. In the spring, the regular decisions on college applications come in. Also, responses to requests for financial aid will be forthcoming. For girls, the invitation to the senior prom can be a source of apprehension and concern.

Watch the newspaper for items of recognition. Sports achievement is the obvious one to watch for, but check community organizations as well. For example, during the high school years, some boys complete their Eagle Scout training. Many other students enter all types of contests and competitions.

Students' Cultures

We're sure you've heard before how important it is to become aware of the ethnic and cultural backgrounds of the people in your classes. This includes not only obvious features, such as race, but also religions, gender, family, and other cultural identity factors. For example, some students will not ask questions when they don't understand an idea or a direction because they have been taught not to bother adults. Questioning is not valued in their families. Students may tell the teacher what he or she wants to hear—yes, they understand an assignment; yes, they can do a math problem. Culture may dictate that they are passive in the classroom rather than active participants.

One way to address this challenge is make an effort to involve each student in class proceedings. One easy system is to write each student's name on a Popsicle-type craft stick and keep the sticks in a can, pulling them out as you need "volunteers." Another idea is to instruct each student who speaks in class to select the person to talk next; however, the rule is that you may only pick someone you don't know very well. This ensures that students don't only call on their friends and other students end up being left out. Regardless of what method you use, it is indeed a challenge to distribute equitably the participation in class so the same loud voices don't always dominate contributions.

Body language differs from group to group. Certain cultures teach that children should look down, averting their eyes as a sign of respect. Other cultures teach that a child should not look away but should look directly into the eyes of the person who is addressing him or her. To avoid problems of communication, the teacher must examine his or her culture and the culture of the students.

As time goes on, you will get to know your students and they will get to know each other through their participation in class activities. Through discussion, writing, and various demonstrations of performance, you will become more and more familiar with each student's personality and his or her needs and interests. Some teachers like to ask students to do collages or fill in a "coat of arms" or answer a set of interview questions. The knowledge you gain will help you in your planning for the future.

Introductions

A good rule of thumb is to model what you expect of others. If you want students to be open and forthcoming in the ways they present themselves, then you should be prepared to do so as well. Students admire teachers who are not only experts in their subject area but who are also compassionate, caring, accessible, and human. If you want students to be open and honest, then you will wish to demonstrate these values in your own behavior as much as possible.

You are about to create and maintain a community in your classroom, one that we hope will be based on mutual respect and trust, a place where it is safe to express ideas, to ask questions, to challenge thinking, to reflect on learning, and to personalize what is presented in meaningful ways. To encourage your students to show the requisite courage needed for contemplative learning and constructive risk taking, you must show them the way through your own behavior.

You may want to begin your classes with some sort of introductory exercise designed to help students learn one another's names, to develop some cohesion and trust, to create a climate of critical inquiry. For example, you might ask students to give their names, with adjectives that describe them whose first letters are the same as their first names. Getting to know your students and helping them to feel comfortable with each other are the first steps toward a successful year.

4 Dressing for Success

Teaching is a performance profession, not unlike that of acting on stage. Our audiences study our costumes and decide, based on these appearances, whether we are convincing in our roles, whether we are even worth listening to. Parents, colleagues, and staff, as well, form strong impressions of our skills and professional competence based on the ways we present ourselves.

In the beginning of the school year, it is especially important to establish yourself as a person worthy of respect. You will want to create an image for the students of someone who is a responsible adult mentor yet someone who is also "with-it" in terms of being able to relate to contemporary fashion styles.

You would only have to go back into your own memories to recall teachers who wore especially clunky shoes, or out-of-style clothing, or inappropriate outfits to realize just how important it is to dress for success. Your clothes tell a story about you, especially to impressionable youth whose identities are so tied up in their clothing.

First Impressions

First impressions convey strong messages. As you glance around the room and check out each of your students, note your own personal reactions to each of them. The girl with the three nose rings and studs through her tongue. The guy with the purple hair. The guy next to him wearing all black. The girl who looks like she just walked out of a fashion magazine. In each case, you form a definite impression and make some preliminary predictions about who you will like and who will be trouble.

Of course, many of these first impressions are inaccurate and misleading. Nevertheless, they do set up certain expectations that are often difficult to alter. For this reason, you will want to give considerable thought to the ways you present yourself to students and staff.

It is important to dress comfortably, especially with regard to shoes because you will be on your feet most of the day. Although high heels might be in fashion for women, a low-heeled shoe will be more practical. Although a flip-flop may be comfortable, it does not offer the same protection as a shoe or a sandal with leather pieces across the front and a sling in the back.

Standards of dress continue to change, even in the business world, where more informal dress is becoming commonplace. You may notice experienced teachers around the school perfectly at ease in their jeans and T-shirts. Some day soon, you, too, may reach a point when you can dress exactly how you prefer. As a beginning, probationary teacher, however, you will be smart to dress the part of the consummate professional: stylish, casual, and conservative rather than flashy. Dress codes vary from district to district and school to school. Check with your administration if you have questions.

Spirit Days

Many schools have spirit days when school colors are worn. Some schools have T-shirts with the school logo. Now, most people wear jeans with a T-shirt, so school spirit days create a problem as to how to dress.

Many female teachers decide to wear the T-shirt with a jean skirt rather than jean pants. Rather than blue jean pants, another color denim, such as black, could be considered. If you do decide to wear jeans, make sure that they are clean and in good condition. You never know when the yearbook staff will be around to take your picture!

Whatever you do, you don't want your clothes to be distracting. Students will talk about what you are wearing rather than what you are saying. If you dress like an older brother or sister, you may be treated like one. If your dress is too formal, the students will comment. Clothing is a visual cue for middle school and high school students; it signals where they are and what purpose is at hand. It tells them what behavior is expected.

It's important to look nice and take pride in how you look.

I (Cary) remember a teacher I had who constantly wore the same two dresses. It seemed like she just switched off every other day. This did not speak well of her personal hygiene. I'm not saying you need a different outfit for each day of the month, but it is good to make sure you avoid wearing the same thing all of the time.

Another teacher I had was extremely outrageous in her appearance, even distracting. She was weird. It was hard to listen to her because of the outfits she would wear. One day, she came to school with a red dot on her forehead like that of an Indian woman. We thought she was making fun of Indian people. We all wondered why she did that, but she never explained herself. Sometimes, she came to school with so much makeup on her face that she looked like a clown. Another time, she wore a red jacket with the Playboy bunny emblem on it. You can tell that we all spent a lot of time talking about stuff she was wearing.

I would advise teachers to definitely have your own style, but to make sure your appearance isn't going to detract from the task at hand. Because, believe me, it's a long year, and we students will be studying every part of you.

Images

Remember the age of your audience. Students develop crushes very easily. I (Ellen) remember one boy who was cutting out paper dolls at the back of the room. I asked him what he was doing. He told me, with more explanation than I wanted to hear: "I'm cutting out paper dolls to dance all over your body." Hopefully, your students will concentrate on your words.

Clothing can also be used to emphasize points you wish to make in teaching. A Spanish teacher may wear a Cinco de Mayo shirt when he introduces Mexican holidays. A humanities teacher may wear a series of T-shirts with impressionist paintings on the front. A geometry teacher could wear a shirt with an Escher design. Even more inventive, an English or history teacher may dress up in period costume to attract student interest in a subject.

The clothing you wear becomes an extension of your whole classroom environment, an expression of your personality. Give serious consideration to the kind of impression you wish to make, and make thoughtful decisions about your wardrobe. After all, you are indeed performing on stage.

5 Beginning and Ending Your Class on the First Day

Your room is ready. You are sporting your single best outfit, the one that positively glows with confidence that you really know what you're doing. You've practiced your welcoming smile over and over, although if truth be told, you wonder how much of your apprehension and uncertainty shows.

You've written your name and room number on the board (to avoid embarrassment for the student who has mistakenly entered the wrong room). You stand at the front of an empty room. The bell rings or chimes or buzzes or belches. You move to the doorway. In they come: students who check you out as they walk by, sizing you up and making their predictions about whether you are boring or fun, mean or nice, an easy mark or street wise to their favorite games.

First Contact

No, this isn't first contact with aliens, but it might feel that way initially. This is the point where you begin, showing confidence and poise, pretending like you know what you're doing.

28

"Welcome everyone!" You smile warmly. "I'm glad to be here, my first day in your school . . . "

The specifics of what you say are less important than the main objective of revealing yourself to the students as someone who does know what you're doing (most of the time), who is warm and caring but also unwilling to tolerate disrespect. If you have a sense of humor, show it. But whatever you do, set the tone for what will follow throughout the year.

Make sure you have their attention when you speak. Project your voice so everyone can hear you. Remind students to check their schedules to make sure they are in the right place at the right time. State your name clearly so students will be able to pronounce it.

Give them some background on who you are, but rather than reciting your credentials, tell them a brief story about how you ended up where you are. You are doing this to reduce your own anxiety level as much as those of the students who are also wondering about what miseries you will subject them to.

Describe your vision of the class—what the content will be, how the time in class will be spent, what the students will accomplish. Be enthusiastic! Let them know you remember what it was like to be a student, that you know it's important that things be fun and exciting. You intend to accommodate them as best you can. Stress what they will be able to do at the end that they can't do now! Let your optimism shine! Your interest and enthusiasm will be contagious.

Move to specifics. List the various activities they will engage in. If you have samples of the types of projects they might do, you could show them at this time. Let them see an example of the textbook, primary documents, and other resources they will use. Explain your role as a teacher. Set your expectations of them as students.

Spend a minute or two on what supplies, if any, they will need—pen or pencil, paper, folder or binder, any other subject-related equipment. Discuss any fees that might have to be paid and the procedures to follow. Realize the students may need a couple of days before they can get to the store to purchase what you have asked for or to get the money for the fees. Not all teachers give the list the first day. Not all parents are able to take their children to the store the first night. Be patient. Be prepared in the meantime for students to come to class empty-handed for the first few days.

Also be prepared to be tested by someone early in your introduction, some student who is looking for attention, who likes to challenge authority, or perhaps someone who is just playful. Don't overreact. Just remain calm, poised, and firm. Show that you have a sense of humor as well, but don't tolerate disrespect.

Movement

You have by now probably reached the limits of how long students can sit quietly without doing something. One of the functions, actually, of the student who acts out is to serve as an alarm clock to let you know that it is time to change the movement, flow, and energy of the class.

Remember, this is the first day of school after vacation. Students have gotten used to their freedom. Most of them resent being back, stuck inside when the weather is still so nice, and there are so many things they would rather be doing. They've also got a lot on their minds that have little to do with your agenda: which boys and girls they might like, pressures at home, work and other responsibilities, parties coming up. Also, they are just plain tired, not used to getting up so early.

There are a variety of things you can do at this point. You can ask them to fill out information cards, as mentioned in a previous chapter. You could also get them involved in some type of introductory activity with partners or in small groups. You can have them interview each other with or without guided questions that you have prepared.

Students can be given a list of questions such as the following to ask a partner.

- Where were you born?
- What is your favorite activity outside of school?
- What is your favorite school subject?
- What is your favorite food?
- What kind of music do you like?
- What is your favorite television program?
- What did you do over summer vacation?
- If you could live anywhere, where would you go?

- If you could meet anyone in history, who would you choose?
- What do you think is the most difficult job?
- Do you have a nickname you prefer to be called?
- What would you like other people to know about you?

Another option is to have students participate in a group consensus activity, such as the following:

In groups of four to six people, find examples of the following items that *every* person in the group likes:

- An item of food
- Television program
- Song or musical artist
- Movie
- Personal characteristic in a friend

Still another variation is to organize a kind of scavenger-hunt-type questionnaire that requires students to interact with others in their search for answers. More simply, you can put them in a circle to get them talking. Whatever you do, however, turn the focus on them in such a way that each person gets the chance to speak.

Setting the Rules

Toward the end of the period, draw the students' attention to the topic of class rules. To achieve the goals for the class, some accommodations will have to be made to ensure that the class runs smoothly. Here, you can review the school rules if you are in a situation where rules for the entire school have been predetermined. If not, you can present the rules you feel are most important. The rule of thumb is to choose five. Or if you choose to be democratic, you can begin discussion with the class.

One creative variation that is somewhat time-consuming (so you may need to include it for the second meeting) is to ask the students to work cooperatively in small groups to invent their own rules. Although initially, their suggestions may be silly and inappropriate ("We don't need any rules!"), you will be amazed at how wisely they will create exactly the guidelines that are needed. Your job in this exercise is to draw out of them their own commitment to follow rules they develop for themselves. This allows you, at a later time, to be able to say to them, "Look, *you* are the ones who decided that nobody should be disrespected in this room. I'm just following through on what you came up with."

However rules are explained, you must let them know what behavior is expected and what will happen if they don't follow them. For example, if you are bothered by students getting up during the period to sharpen pencils, then tell them, "Pencils should be sharpened before the bell rings. Otherwise, you'll be writing with dull points."

Some Sample Rules

Think of the rule setting as constructive discipline. You are setting a behavior code that will avoid conflict in the future and provide the students with an environment in which they will be ready to learn. Following are some examples of the kinds of rules that you might consider implementing:

Students should be in their seats when the tardy bells rings. If the tardy is to be excused or not counted, the student must have a pass. Otherwise, the student must report to the dean or principal's office.

Homework is due at the beginning of the period. The alternative, of course, is that the students will do it during class and turn it in at the middle or at the end of the period. Some teachers prefer to have the homework turned in or placed in a basket before the tardy bell rings.

Textbooks are to be brought to class every day. This rule must be stressed, especially for students who come from different countries where procedures are different.

Raise your hand and wait to be recognized before speaking. By the secondary level, most students understand the reason for and are used to the practice of this necessary rule. However, after a break from school, students need to be reminded.

Book covers must be used on all texts. If you ask that the students cover their books, they will remain in better shape and last longer. Also this gives them an acceptable place to doodle, and the desk tops will stay cleaner (we hope). The students can change the book covers to fit their moods.

Be courteous and considerate to all students and faculty. Review manners and etiquette. Swearing will not be tolerated. Name-calling is not permitted. An atmosphere of respect will prevail.

Class Syllabus

If your class syllabus is available, a logical next step would be to pass it out. Otherwise, present the main ideas. First, identify the specific course objectives. Then, slowly and carefully review the general policies. Explain the requirements for the class and the evaluation system. The grading scale should be clearly stated. The attendance and makeup procedures should be carefully explained so as to prevent problems in the future. Set a firm policy on the completion of makeup work and tests. Inform students of your policy on work turned in late. Will it be corrected? Will it be graded? The syllabus sets the framework for the class proceedings. It is worthwhile to commit time and effort into its construction. It will be read and used by students, parents, and the administration

Get to Work

If there is any time left, start a lesson. Believe it or not, most experienced teachers can get through all the steps mentioned previously and still save some time to begin work. We are not saying that that is a reasonable expectation for a beginner, but at the very least, be prepared to get into a lesson. You will feel reassured there will be no dead time.

In your fist lesson, be creative and clever. Teach something new that presumes they have no knowledge of the subject. Or pose a stimulating question related to your subject. "Did you know . . ?" "What do you think of . . . ?" Let them leave with something they didn't have when they walked in the door—a new idea, a skill, an interest, a piece of information, an "itch that needs scratching."

Closure

Don't let the bell end your class; *you* end it, by timing your final words before the bell rings. Advise students to leave in an orderly way. Remind them if there is any homework due. Say goodbye with a smile. Show them you are looking forward to seeing them the next day. Make eye contact or say a few words to as many kids as you can when they file out of the room.

Time Considerations

If you are on an abbreviated schedule on the first day of school and your first meeting with the students is a short one, then two adaptations to this plan are suggested. First, wait to review the syllabus until the second day. You may have additional students enrolling on the first day, and they might not appear until the second day anyhow. Instead of handling the details, use a short get-acquainted activity in which the students work in pairs or in small groups. Your main goal is simply that they will leave their first contact with you saying to themselves (and one another): "Hey, that teacher's pretty cool. That class could be interesting."

A Cheat Sheet

I (Jeffrey) was so terrified before I taught my first class that I actually wrote out a "cheat sheet" of notes for myself because I thought for sure I would forget one of the 2,000 different things I wanted to remember. Once I was in class, I found I didn't really need it because a student immediately asked a question that got us going in a completely different direction. But the idea of bringing notes or an outline with you is a good idea.

Following is a lesson plan for "Day One:"

Welcome

> State your name.
> Identify the room and subject.

Introduction of Yourself

> Say who you are and where you came from.
> Tell about how you came to be a teacher.
> Mention interests related to the subject and outside of school.

Introduction to the Class

> Describe the topics of study.
> List typical activities.
> Show a sample of projects or products.
> Show the textbook.

Introducing the Students to
Each Other Through an Activity

> Have students share outcomes with the class or collect written responses.

Class Rules

> Present them.
> Structure time for students to develop their own rules.

Distribution of the Syllabus

A Quick Lesson

Dismissal-Goodbye

6 Managing Paperwork

And you thought teaching was mostly about direct instruction and interactions with students. If only that were so.

Secondary school teachers are besieged with paperwork, and you had better organize yourself from the beginning or you will never catch up. There are daily attendance rosters to manage, not to mention reports to various offices, lesson plans written in which you pretend to know what you might end up doing in the future, homework assignments to read and check off, papers to grade, tests to create and score. The list goes on and on.

We don't mean to be discouraging, just realistic. Paperwork doesn't have to get you down if you are well-organized, efficient, and sensible in the ways you operate.

Attendance

Taking attendance is the least of your paperwork problems. After all, it just takes a few minutes each day and helps you to learn each student's name. One teacher we know considers this task an utter waste of time, not to mention a rather inefficient way to learn names (he has a terrible memory). Instead, what he does is videotape the class, one student at a time, as they say their names and something brief about themselves.

He can then study the tape on his own time, drilling hi
memorize names. Students are thus *very* impressed that he
attendance after the first few days simply by scanning the room.

Another unique way to take attendance is with a specially designed
board in the front of the room. Each student has an assigned magnet
that is kept in a column up on the board. As students enter the room
each day, they see a question written on the board with several possible
answers. These questions can relate to the subject matter or even be
more playful, as the following examples show:

The question: My favorite fast food restaurant is
The choices: McDonald's   Wendy's   Burger   Taco Bell
                                        King

The question: I think O. J. Simpson was
The choices: Innocent   Guilty   Temporarily   A great
                                    insane   football player

The question: The Nile River is located on which continent:
The choices: Asia   Africa   Antarctica   Australia

Each day, you would make up a different question for students to
consider as they entered the room. They would then remove their
individual magnets and place it in one of the columns. The names
leftover are those who are absent. You can even begin class with a
discussion of the question that you asked.

Grades

As a classroom teacher, you will frequently receive requests for students'
grades, whether it is from a counselor, a parent, a dean, or the student.
In a formal way, many secondary schools send out progress reports
indicating "unsatisfactory progress" midway through a card-marking
period. Athletic and activity (spirit leader, band) eligibility checks take
place regularly, too. Therefore, it becomes very important to have the
grading up to date. For this purpose, a computer grading program is strongly
recommended. Programs such as Micrograde are easy to use and compute the averages as soon as grades are entered into the computer.

The computer programs are flexible and allow you to design your
own standards based on whatever categories you prefer (participation,

class work, homework, projects, quizzes, tests) and whatever weighting system you would like (points, percentages). They will even compute extra-credit work in the average. Furthermore, if you have access to a printer, the programs allow you to print a report of a student's grades very quickly. It is helpful to have this information for reports you submit on the students and to give to parents at conferences.

Many districts now allow teachers to turn in the computer pages as formal records rather than the traditional grade book.

Most teachers are still required to turn in a traditional grade book. The designers of these pages run very small lines horizontally, in sets of two or three, across the page. This works fine if all you are doing is keeping attendance. Then, you can easily use one line for each student.

Although the lines may be numbered, I (Ellen) ignore the printed numbers. On the top line, I print the student's name and mark attendance. Then, I use the next two (or three or more depending on how many categories you have) for grades. For example, the second line is used for test and quiz grades. The third line is used for homework and class work. On the fourth line, I keep a running average and notes to myself to indicate places and people the student visited other than my class (field trip, nurse, dean, test). It is too hard to squeeze all the information in on one line. The advantage of this system is that when a student is missing a grade, you can quickly see if it was due to negligence or due to an absence. Some schools will require a page for attendance only and subsequent pages for grades. Then, you may have no choice.

Students can be taught to keep track of their own grades and compute their own averages. You need to explain the weighting system and give examples. Many teachers provide forms for the students to use throughout the card-marking period.

Paperwork Considerations

One of the major mistakes common to beginning teachers is giving too many written assignments. Remember: You are making as much work for yourself as you are for your students. Each paper or assignment must be read, evaluated, graded, recorded, then the grades averaged. All of this can be very time-consuming. Some of you may even wish to have some sort of life outside of school.

There are a number of things you can consider as ways to reduce your workload:

Always consider the merit of the assignment. Is it really necessary, to accomplish the larger goals you are after? There is nothing that turns students off more than busy work in which they can't see how it will help them in some constructive way.

Can the assignment be self-graded or self-evaluated? Because the purpose of many assignments is to give students systematic practice in new concepts and skills and then to integrate feedback into their future learning, there is no reason why you have to be the one who does all the evaluating. Post the correct answers on the board, and let students review their own answers. Occasionally, you can spot-check for accuracy with warnings that if students make too many mistakes in their self-corrections, they will lose all credit.

Can the assignment be completed as a group or paired activity? This is one way to cut the number of papers in half. Students may also benefit from the cooperative effort, assuming they each participate equally.

Does the assignment need to be graded at all? Sometimes, constructive comments and corrections are all that is needed, rather than a grade.

It isn't always necessary to collect homework assignments each day. Sometimes, a weekly or biweekly homework check may be sufficient, in which case, the students are responsible for maintaining their own paperwork.

Control the length of the assignments to reasonable limits. Do this both for the students' benefit and to manage your own available time.

Vary the type of assignments and evaluation methods you use. Do this not only to give students a chance to demonstrate different skills but also to create variety for yourself.

Rather than just requiring written assignments, be creative. Design performance or project assignments that can show mastery of the material. Students can create dioramas, plays, posters, or videos.

Share the load. An interdisciplinary approach would have one teacher evaluate an assignment for content (e.g., science, social studies) while another evaluates for technical writing skills (English).

Use aides, if available. Many schools provide student aides for teachers. Often, you will be able to create assignments that the aides can correct if not grade. With the use of computer grading programs, aides can be taught to enter grades on the computer for quick averaging.

Decide on the best time for you to examine student assignments. Some teachers are able to get most of their work done during preparation periods. Others remain in their rooms after school so they can go home without anything else to worry about. Still others prefer to relax for awhile and complete their paperwork at night or early in the morning. Whatever structure you prefer, stick with a consistent program so you are able to keep on top of things.

Be punctual in returning assignments to students.

I (Cary) remember one time how hard I worked for a certain grade in Math class. Needing an "A" to achieve a good grade for the quarter, I spent countless hours reviewing the material. After taking the test, I turned it in to the teacher confidently. As my next math class approached, I got really excited waiting to get my test back. I really needed that reward to keep my momentum going because the next lesson was really hard.

I showed up for class the next day and was surprised the teacher said nothing about returning our tests. When I asked him what was going on, he said he'd have them ready the next day. Again I waited not so patiently, and again the same thing happened. A whole week went by, and still we never got the tests back. Finally, I got up the nerve to ask the teacher again; this time, he yelled at me to stop bugging him.

About a week and a half after taking the test, we finally got the test back, and I received my "A." But it didn't seem to matter any more. We were already on to other stuff, and I cut back on my study time because I had no idea how I was doing in the class.

When kids work hard for tests, they deserve to get their grades back as soon as possible. Whatever you do, don't lie by telling them they'll have their tests back within 2 days and not give them back for a week. If you are going to have problems grading the tests right away, tell the kids so they will know what to expect. Better yet, get the grades back to us as soon as you can. We need to know how we're doing in your classes.

The Mailbox

Along with the things you initiate for your students to complete will be paperwork required by the school. Some days, it seems impossible to keep your mailbox empty. Every time you go by, there will be something in it for you to peruse—endless notices, announcements, requests for information, forms to fill out, plus the countless catalogues and letters from text and instructional materials companies.

In the beginning, it is wise to look carefully at the papers that are placed in your mailbox. Once you become familiar with the types of information you receive, you will be able to categorize and prioritize your responses. Daily announcements will be stuffed in mailboxes everyday, usually at about the same time. Scan these as you post them for the information that pertains to you or your students. An announcement of a forthcoming assembly (with the bell schedule for that day) can be posted for reference later in the week. College visits and college scholarship announcements can be posted in addition to competitions that are coming up. Each day, you can refer your students to the latest additions to the bulletin board.

In the Beginning

Just as students are advised to use daily planners in study skills classes, we suggest that a calendar will be helpful to you as well. The first weeks of the fall semester will be especially busy. There are several tasks that must be completed right away. A syllabus needs to be written for each class. Most schools require these to be submitted to an administrator. Emergency lesson plans will have to be written as well. Once they are completed, they must also be updated from time to time.

Requests for information are very common at the beginning of the year as administrators check on the numbers of students, textbooks, desks, and other equipment. These forms are often placed in the mailboxes in the morning and usually have a quick turnaround time—the end of the school day. Also, there will be information sheets to be posted—fire drill procedures, suspension rules, no food or drink in the classroom, and the like. The good news is that the amount of paperwork will decrease as time goes on.

Certain forms are distributed on a regular basis. You can mark your calendar for yourself so you know when to expect them and when they are due back to a particular office. For example, athletic and activity eligibility forms are distributed on a regular schedule and due back to an office by a specific time. Some schools require these every week; others may only want them every third week. This means your grade averaging has to be kept up to date. Some teachers make a notation in their grade books as to which students play a given sport or participate in a given activity. Then, they scan the list of names and check the grade averages for those students. Other teachers find this information distracting in the grade books, so they circle the names on the lists that are given to each teacher and just check the circled names against the grade averages in their grade books.

Unsatisfactory progress report forms are distributed at some point in the middle of the grading period. Teachers usually have several days to complete them. You can check the dates, usually with the registrar or the principal's secretary. Progress reports may also be requested for certain students on a weekly basis. These forms may come from the student, parent, counselor, special education teacher, dean, school social worker, or school psychologist.

Some schools have teachers complete daily attendance rosters. The forms are in the mailboxes in the morning and have to be turned in at the end of the day. Suspension lists and withdrawals are posted daily. The teacher usually has a part in the withdrawal process—checking in textbooks and indicating withdrawal in the grade book, which is a legal document. You may also have to sign a form. A good procedure to follow is to check the lists against your record book at the end of the day before you turn in your attendance.

Excused-absence lists are irregularly distributed, so you have to be on the look out for these. Students may be excused for competitions, assembly preparation, sport events, field trips, and other programs. Several tests are administered throughout the year for different groups of students. You might consider marking these on your calendar, too, so you will know why students are absent.

At the End

It's hard to believe, with everything you are trying to remember in just getting started in the job, but there will come a time when the academic year ends. Unfortunately, this brings another rash of forms to fill out and paperwork to complete.

At the end of each semester, you will need to post schedules for final exams. There will be forms for you to fill out regarding your preferences for teaching next year, textbook needs and supplies for next year, maintenance requests for your room over the track or summer. Various evaluation forms will be requested.

Teachers with senior students will have to report semester grades and fines. They may be involved in distributing graduation-related material, such as senior rings, caps and gowns, and invitations. This is the time for recommendations, resumes, and senior projects. Do not agree to review a resume or write a letter of recommendation if the student does not give you enough time—at least a week.

Catalogues, brochures, and letters to teachers will find their way to you. It will take a little while in the beginning to look at the new products that are being offered. But as time goes on, you will be able to determine which companies have books or products that are worth your consideration for a particular course. Check with other teachers and your department head for their opinions. File the catalogues by class or by publisher until you are in a position to request an order.

All of this paperwork may seem overwhelming in the beginning. It is really just the first few weeks and the last few weeks of the year that things seem particularly hectic. Before you become frustrated, remember that almost all professional jobs in contemporary life have their fair share of forms and paperwork to complete. This is just the price we pay for the privilege of doing the fun stuff.

Avoiding Boredom— Theirs and Yours 7

If there's one thing that kids hate most about school (besides having to get up early), it's the boredom. I (Cary) think that most teachers are so repetitive and predictable. Whether it's taking notes or doing problems on the board, the same routines are used over and over again.

My advice is: AVOID THIS! Take risks by trying new ideas. If students come to class and they already know they're going to be lectured to all period, then interest is lost before things even begin.

The way to get my attention (and keep me from falling asleep) is to surprise me. Be innovative and enthusiastic. Catch me off guard, and I will respond positively. Last of all, never act like you are bored. When I can see my teacher is bored, it is definitely going to rub off on me.

The following situation seems to happen too often.

I walk into my science classroom passing a hanging skeleton and all the usual posters of plants and animals. The bell rings, and I take my seat. Well, first I talk to a few of my friends.

The teacher takes attendance and then walks over to the light switch, turning it off. You can hear groans across the room. He turns the overhead projector on and begins the usual hour of nonstop talking. The classroom is dark and stuffy. In the background, I hear the teacher's monotone explaining something. What was that he just said? My head droops, and I feel the coolness of the table against my face. I'm drifting away.

I'm sorry, but in that situation, I could really care less whether a fish has a three-chambered heart or a four-chambered heart.

Who cares?

Entering my history class after lunch, I noticed my teacher was not in the room. Every day, I looked forward to this class as my teacher makes the past come alive. The bell rang and still no teacher. A friend and I started talking about the fight that happened at lunch, as did most of my other classmates. Suddenly, the door was whisked open, and my usually jovial teacher has a sullen look on his face. "Everybody, shut up right now!" he yells.

There was complete silence.

Now, this is weird. This teacher never yells at us. A girl started to giggle, and my teacher screamed at her, "Get out of this classroom right now!"

During the next several minutes, two more kids were thrown out of the classroom for the dumbest reasons—one was chewing gum; the other forgot her pen. He screamed at the gum chewer, who was on the verge of tears: "Get out of here! The gum always ends up on the floor."

As the teacher paced the room, none of us even breathed. We were terrified, as much by how strange this was as by how cruel he was being to us. The teacher walked to the door, opened it, and directed all the students in the hallway (there were now 7 or 8 of them by then) to go to the dean's office. Then he went back to his desk and asked someone a question that nobody knew the answer to. He stormed out of the room claiming he can't teach kids who are as stupid as we are.

We all sat there in silence wondering what happened to our wonderful teacher. A few minutes later, he entered the room bringing all of the kids back. Strangely, he had his usual smile on his face. What the heck is going on?

The teacher explained that what he was doing was acting out the role of a dictator. We had been studying World War II and learning about the ways Hitler and Mussolini had been able to control the populace. The rest of the period, we were so charged up about what we had experienced that none of us wanted to leave when the bell rang. Now, that is teaching.

What Cary described in these two examples is typical of what so many children experience in school. It isn't that they aren't interested in learning, it's just that they don't want to learn what you are teaching or at least by the way you are presenting the material to them. All human beings learn best when they are actively engaged with the content, when they see the relevance of the subject to their lives, when they can imagine specific ways that investing their time and energy will result in something useful and practical. Your job, then, is to keep children, and yourself, excited about what is going on in your classroom. Find a connection that relates to them personally.

Capturing and Maintaining Interest

Long-term planning will help you see the picture of what students experience in the classroom. Take note of your teaching methods. Using a variety of instructional methods and assessments will provide you and your students with needed stimulation. In the following list are several ways to fan the flames of interest.

Imagine yourself as a director, and let the children be the actors. You create a stage, give them a setting, and let them write the script and be the stars. They will shine as they present plays, whether to you individually or to their fellow students.

Involve the students. They can develop interviews, plays, or simulations of events. They can produce projects such as journals, books, newspapers, displays, or products. Ask them to write a jingle, an advertisement, or a song. For example, students in Spanish can demonstrate a conversation between a student and a counselor. Math students can role play the use of an algebra problem. History students can make a magazine of events about a cultural issue. Child development students can create a poster to demonstrate safety issues for toddlers. Home economics students can plan a restaurant and create a menu. Geography students can write songs to describe environments and cultures they have studied. Students teach each other.

Decorate. Change your room. Rearrange the furniture. Create new bulletin boards that correspond to the current topic of study. Decorate your chalk or dry-erase boards. Use crepe paper streamers or balloons for that extra emphasis. Bring in lamps to change the lighting. Just create an atmosphere of the unexpected so that students are kept on their toes.

Illustrate your subject. Use diagrams, pictures, slides, models. Create your own art work. Use charts. Make cartoons. Show photographs. Bring in samples. Play music. Show movies.

I (Jeffrey) experimented with using a "film laboratory" last semester in which students were allowed to pick a selection of movies from the video shelves related to themes of multicultural diversity. I wanted to sensitize them more to other people's experiences; more than that, however, I wanted them to bring the subject into their personal lives.

They not only had to watch movies with a multicultural theme (*White Man's Burden; Six Degrees of Separation; Once Were Warriors; Priscilla, Queen of the Desert; Dangerous Minds,* etc.), but they had to see them in the company of at least three members of their family or friends. Then the students had to lead a discussion with the group about what the films triggered in terms of significant issues.

Instigate questions. Bring in a big box or a big bag, and clear away the space around it. Put a question mark on the front. Let the students guess what is in it. Surprise them with an interesting artifact. Use inquiry as a method of teaching.

Inscribe thought-provoking quotes. Questions or statements can be posed for students' reactions. They can serve as the basis of a journal entry, a brief discussion, or a way to divide the class into teams. They can be posted on the front board or written on a bulletin board. Students can be given the responsibility for providing the "quote of the day" or the "quotes of the week."

Introduce variety. Other activities might be to assign each student a famous person to research or provide a biography about. Take turns letting the rest of the members of the class ask questions to find the identity of the person. Schedule brief reports throughout the week. Set up a round-robin or debate schedule. Use cooperative learning strategies.

Videotape performances of the students, and play them back for the class. Not only do students enjoy seeing themselves on tape, but the tape can be used periodically for review. Also, it provides feedback to students on their communication skills.

Integrate with other disciplines. Art (science, math, physical education) does not have to stand alone as a separate entity. Bring in art work associated with your subject. Play music for the students. Provide for movement when you can. Coordinate your lessons with other members of your faculty. Many middle schools today are organized in teams, which will facilitate the planning process. In other situations, you will need to find people who are interested in joining in collaborative efforts.

Incorporate carefully planned games. Prepare questions and answers in advance for a game of Jeopardy or Tic Tac Toe. Try baseball or football. If you have a behaviorally responsible class, you can even play volleyball with a nerf ball, where the right to serve is earned by correctly answering a question. A simulated Pictionary game will serve to review vocabulary words in German class or in a science class. Students can play as an entire class or in teams of four. The latter, of course, will be noisy, but as you circulate around the room, you will see the level of involvement will be quite high. Games are excellent ways to review material and reinforce knowledge.

Invite guest speakers and parents to your room to share their real-life experiences. Encourage students to find people who are especially interesting and can talk about how a particular subject relates to their lives. An insurance actuary actually made probability theory seem interesting. A Vietnamese immigrant talked about how she views the English language. A homeless person told his story about losing control over his life. Bring the real world into your classroom.

Initiate correspondence. Arrange for a pen pal for your students, as a class or with individuals. This can be in your own school, with another school within your district, or a school in another part of the country or the world. Many students are successfully communicating through E-mail. The Peace Corps will match a teacher with a Peace Corps volunteer through their program called World Wise Schools. They will also provide information on retired volunteers living in your area who are interested in getting involved with your students.

Use multiple resources. Bring in library books and CD-ROMs as well as videotapes. Screen videotapes, and show only the sections that are meaningful. Arrange for students to have access to the Internet. Plan for students to go on field trips.

Include rewards. Build fun into your classroom every week, especially with activities that are seen as rewards for hard work. Students also react positively to prizes. Typically, teachers use candy, but there can be problems such as food allergies and candy wrappers on the floor. Although giving prizes all the time can be costly and may lose meaning, bestowing awards of some type from time to time will get the students' attention. The gift can be an honor as well as a tangible item. Many teachers have effectively used tokens that they distribute and later collect for extra points, free homework passes, or other rewards that their particular students find desirable.

Attitude and Values

As we say throughout this book, the specifics of what you do are not as important as your general attitude and basic values. If you believe that learning should be fun as well as hard work, that humor and play are important parts of school, then boredom will be kept at bay. The elements of surprise, laughter, spontaneity, variability, and high energy can be customized to fit your unique personality and teaching style.

Eating Lunch 8

There are usually several choices in a school as to where to eat lunch, and the decision is not merely one related to ingesting food. Lunch is where a lot of informal networking goes on, where friends are made, where gossip and information are traded, where political alliances are formed, and even where mentoring takes place. It is a time to debrief and support one another. It is also about the only time during the hectic day in which you can talk to adults about what is going on in your life.

Choices, Choices

Whereas you could elect to use your lunch period to catch up on work or simply recover in solitude from the morning's stress, we strongly recommend that as a newcomer to the school community, you use all available opportunities to forge new relationships. For that reason, it might even be a good idea for you to experiment with as many different lunch settings as you can, making the rounds, so to speak, before you eventually settle on a few locales.

Your decision about where to eat lunch will depend on several factors: the cuisine available and whether it suits your taste and budget, whether the setting is a comfortable environment for you, and most important, who is in attendance and how they treat you. Some groups you join may virtually ignore you or even act somewhat put off that you are attempting to join a relatively intact culture. Other groups may be somewhat cautious and suspicious, watching you carefully to see if you are their kind of person in terms of basic values and personality. Trust us, though: Somewhere around the school are other individuals and groups that would be utterly delighted to have you join them. You just have to take the time to investigate what options are available.

The most obvious place to eat is in the teachers' dining room. This is usually adjacent to the school cafeteria. Often, there is a menu tailored to adult tastes. In some schools, most teachers gather there, whether they have brought lunches or not.

In newer schools, each department may have a workroom that attracts the staff members from that area. In other schools, there are various workrooms or lounges spaced throughout the building(s), where teachers gather.

At one school, I (Ellen) found a group of teachers who identified themselves as the "upstairs lunch bunch." This was a mixed group of people from different departments who met in a spacious workroom. Word of mouth brought people to the location, as it was a lively group. There were microwaves to use if you brought a lunch; otherwise, you could walk to the cafeteria to buy food and bring it upstairs. It was far from my classroom but worth the walk for the spirited conversations that took place.

Most schools will have a group that likes to play cards for relaxation. Choices will range from bridge to poker. Others play Trivial Pursuit. Some have televisions going for the news or soap operas.

As must be readily apparent, teachers group themselves together during lunch according to a number of variables: the geographic proximity of their rooms, their ages (older and younger), their political or lifestyle beliefs, their teaching specialties, their physical or social attractiveness, to mention just a few. You will find it fascinating research just to observe the various groups in action and try to figure out what bonds them together.

Things also become complicated when you have multiple interests and roles in the school. If you coach a sport but do not teach physical education classes, you have to decide whether to eat with the coaches, your department, or a group of friends.

From time to time, you may enjoy eating lunch with the students. Visit the cafeteria. Sit down with a group. Or invite them to bring their lunches to your room. You'll have a chance to talk to them informally. Let them lead the conversation. Let them ask you questions. Learn about their worlds by listening rather than controlling the conversation. Sometimes, they might even forget you are a teacher, or even an adult, and a whole new world will open up before your eyes and ears in which you will really get a feeling for what it's like to be a teenager again.

The Consequences of the Decision

Regardless of the place you choose, you will want to consider carefully the consequences of your decision. Some groups are notorious for the complaining and whining that goes on. It can be very depressing to hear adults berate the students and their parents day in and day out. Some people can be quite cynical about the state of education and the teaching profession. Each and every lunch period is spent taking turns complaining about how awful things are in the school, how unmotivated and unruly the kids are today, and how nonsupportive the administration is. Then, particular staff members are selected to bash and gossip about. Even if some of the complaints and criticisms are true, a new teacher does not need to be subjected to such negative energy in the middle of the day. Furthermore, such teachers will not want to have someone like you around who is so upbeat and enthusiastic; their atmosphere thrives on pessimism.

Other lunch groups get together to do strategic planning. Science teachers plan a field trip. Two teachers plan an interdisciplinary unit: The social studies teacher targets the beginning of a unit on the Great Depression when the junior English teacher assigns *The Grapes of Wrath* by John Steinbeck. Teachers brainstorm new ideas, share techniques that work, take pride in their successes. They exchange ideas on classroom management and discipline or even compare notes about what works with some students who are particularly tough to handle.

Some lunch groups develop a norm in which any school-related conversation is prohibited. These teachers prefer to talk instead about their personal lives, their families and friends, social and political events, books and movies, community activities. Such individuals prefer to get away from school for a little while; they want to know one another, not as teachers but as human beings.

Every school will have its own options available, not just centered around larger groups but even smaller arrangements of two and three teachers who get together. As much as you will feel the attraction to settle down by yourself or with another new teacher you have befriended, force yourself to reach out to others. Even if you later decide you'd rather eat alone or with one friend, you will at least have circulated enough within the school to know what options are available.

Final Advice

Wherever you eat lunch, don't try to grade papers or take care of other paper work. Many teacher unions worked very hard to get a "duty free" lunch, and you may be reproached by colleagues, some gently and some not so gently, if you bring papers to work on or even mail to read during lunch.

You must build into your day some structures that will keep you mentally alert and physically nourished. There are few jobs as exhausting as that of a high school teacher. The lunch period is a critical time for you to replenish your energy, both nutritionally and emotionally, before you once again jump back into the fray.

Connecting
With Students   9

In spite of all the training you've had in teaching methods, technology, use of materials, and classroom management, it is through your relationships with students that you affect and influence them most dramatically. You would only have to recall your own most important mentors and effective teachers to realize that it wasn't the stuff they knew that was so important, or how brilliant they were as lecturers, or how skilled they were in organizing their lessons; rather, it was who they were as human beings. Somehow, some way, they were able to connect with you so that you felt respected and cared for. You weren't *just* a student to them; you were someone who really mattered.

The connection you felt to your best teachers was built on trust and caring. These were people in your life who seemed to be able to reach you at a core level. They nourished not only your mind but also your heart and spirit. During times when you were most impressionable, perhaps even most vulnerable, these teachers were there for you. With them in your corner, you didn't feel so misunderstood, so confused, so alone.

Being Visible and Accessible

I've (Ellen) often wondered whether the most good I've done at school was in the hallways rather than in the classroom. It is during class

55

changes that I make contact with as many students as I can, offer an encouraging few words or a smile. I try to make myself as visible as I can in the school, so that kids get used to seeing me visiting their worlds rather than always staying in my own classroom. During my preparation period, I will visit the art room or the science room, for example. I want students to know that I really care about them, and I do this by making myself as accessible as I can.

Many students spend more quality time with their teachers in any given day than they do with their own parents. With so many parents working—working more than one job—students today often seek out a teacher to talk to when something is bothering them before or after school. The range of topics is extreme. You never know when a student will approach you with "Can I talk to you for a minute?" It will usually be more than a minute, and you never know what the subject will be. Usually, it will be when no one else is around, which means at the end of the day when you are ready to go home.

- "I just found out I'm pregnant. What should I do?"
- "My dad took off, and we don't know when he's coming back. I'm not sure I even care."
- "I was thinking of dropping out of school. I really need to earn some more money."
- "I think I've got a drinking problem. I don't know. Probably not, but I've been blacking out lately."
- "My boyfriend wants to break up with me. Isn't there some way I can deal with this?"
- "There's this girl I like in your sixth hour class. How do you think I could approach her?"
- "I have no idea what college I should go to, or even if I should go to college at all."
- "I've been so depressed that lately, I've been thinking about . . . you know . . . maybe . . . hurting myself."
- "I can't concentrate lately. On anything."

In each of these examples, students are connecting with you. More than asking for advice or counseling, they are saying they trust you. You are one of the few adults in their lives who they trust enough to confide their most pressing problems to, their most confusing struggles.

Your job, of course, is not to solve their problems, which you have little time for, nor even to serve as their counselor, which you have little training for. Instead, you are using your relationships with students to be a good listener, to support them, to encourage them to make sound decisions, in some cases, to get some help and make an appropriate referral. But you will be amazed what you can do for kids simply by connecting with them, letting them know that you really care.

Listen, Don't Talk

In connecting with students, your primary role is as a listener, not a talker, and especially not an advice giver. In fact, in some instances, giving advice to kids is about the worst thing you can do. If things don't work out the way they hoped, they will blame you for the rest of their lives. Even worse, if the advice you offer does work out well, you have taught them to depend on you (or other adults) in the future. You have reinforced the idea that they don't know what's best for themselves and can't make their own decisions.

Rather than telling students what to do with their lives, and you certainly will have some rather strong opinions on any issue, you should instead concentrate on building a strong connection in which they feel heard and understood by you. There are certain skills used by counselors, called "active listening," that you may want to get some training in when you have the time. Essentially, these skills help you to communicate your interest and then reflect back what you've heard in such a way that the other person can work out the problem.

It is more your ongoing relationships with students, rather than any specific guidance you offer, that will make the greatest difference. You don't have the time or the training to do any real counseling—besides, there are professionals in your school who have been specifically trained for that work. But within short periods of time, you can help your students feel supported and understood. At times, you can even encourage them to work toward small, realistic, incremental goals that are in the directions they would like to go. More than anything else, however, just try to make strong connections. You will be amazed how healing a supportive relationship can be.

Reach Out to Students

One way you help students to personalize your subject area to their lives is to continuously make connections to what matters most to them. Use examples related to sports, contemporary music, current events. Better yet, ask students to articulate ways that what you're doing relates to their lives.

Outside of your class, make a point to visit students where they hang out. Attend athletic contests. Be seen at sporting events. Go to school competitions. Volunteer to be a chaperon at school dances.

Teachers frequently call home to talk to parents. One secret is to call home just to talk to the student. The conversation is private. The other students don't see or hear you targeting a classmate for a reprimand or for praise, either of which can be equally embarrassing to the student.

I (Ellen) have done this unintentionally, trying to reach a parent for help regarding uncooperative behavior, for example, and have ended up talking to the student when the parent wasn't home. I told him I was calling regarding his behavior and asked him to relay a message to his parents. I found my mission was accomplished.

You can also make a point to call students at home, not just when they are in trouble but when they've done something you especially appreciate. Tell students when you are proud of them, when you've seen some improvement in their work, when you've noticed some extra effort extended, or just that you've been thinking about them.

In addition to making phone calls, you can also write notes to students. In such brief communications, you can give them encouragement and support, make suggestions for books you think they might like, or even take the time to say some things privately that might be helpful for them to hear.

Some Quick Interventions

If you have taken the time to develop solid relationships with your students, then it is far more likely they will be open to necessary interventions you must employ.

One time, I (Ellen) turned around to see Howard with his arms around a girl from behind, trying to reach his pencil. Howard is a playful young teenager who likes to get attention from the girls. This time, however, his behavior could have been interpreted as sexual harassment. When I called him to my desk, he quickly broke his hold on the girl and came to talk to me. I very privately and quietly brought to his attention that this behavior could be misinterpreted. I tried to tell him this in a way that was less a censure than a good-natured "word to the wise." He was open to this feedback because he trusted me and knew I wasn't putting him down; I was really trying to help him.

This interaction could easily have turned out differently. Some students will take offense or feel threatened by invasions of their privacy. You can extend yourself to students and reach out all you can, but ultimately, they will let you know if and when they are ready to respond to your overtures.

A Review of Things to Remember
When Connecting With Students

- Listen carefully without interrupting.
- Listen not only for what the student is saying but also for what is being implied beneath the surface.
- Stay neutral and don't judge the student, or trust may be breached.
- Communicate with your body, face, eyes, your whole being, that you are intensely interested in what students are saying.
- Show compassion and empathy in your manner and style.
- Whenever possible, don't let yourself be interrupted or distracted when a student is confiding in you.
- Prove that you've understood what was said by occasionally responding with reflections of feeling and content that you heard.
- Avoid giving advice or telling students what to do with their lives.
- Make yourself as visible and accessible as you can.
- If you must ask questions, don't interrogate kids; instead, ask open-ended inquiries that encourage them to elaborate.
- Look carefully for signs of severe distress; if a student does seem to be in danger of harm or abuse, you must report it to the administration.

- At the end of a conversation, summarize what you heard and ask the student to do the same.
- Make appropriate referrals to the counselor or other professionals when a student could profit from such help.
- Follow up on the conversations by remembering to ask students how they're doing and what they've done since you last talked.

Connecting With Difficult Students

In spite of your best intentions, there will be a number of students who don't respond to your noble overtures. Don't let them get you down. As a beginning teacher, you are often assigned to some of the most challenging groups of kids, those who are unmotivated or somewhat difficult to handle.

Although all teachers wouldn't necessarily share the same definition of who a difficult student is, there is some consensus as to which ones may challenge you the most in your efforts to reach them:

- The angry student looks sullen, with a chip on his shoulder. No matter what you do, he will resist your efforts.
- The withdrawn student is certainly not a behavior problem; quite the opposite, she may sit passively in the back of the room or even sleep with her head on the desk.
- The quiet student just doesn't talk at all. He may or may not be paying attention; you really can't tell. No matter what you do to try and draw him out, he is so shy that he just smiles enigmatically.
- The student who is in over her head feels like she is so far behind there is no point in even trying to cooperate in your class. She has given up all hope.
- The procrastinator continually plays games with you. He always has excuses for why he doesn't have his work completed. He may be wickedly charming, but he manages to avoid doing much that is useful.

- The addicted student is strung out on drugs or alcohol. Her attention is, at best, fleeting. She sits in the back of the room with a glassy-eyed stare.
- The overly social student is always flirting or disturbing others around him. You stop him a dozen times, but he doesn't seem to respond to the corrections.
- The class clown may be motivated by either a sense of humor or something more perverse. Regardless of his intentions, he is constantly the center of attention.

We could go on a *lot* longer with our list. In fact, competitions among teachers as to who has the most annoying, disruptive, difficult students is a frequent topic of conversation in some lunch groups. We don't mean to frighten you with the idea that you will encounter so many kids who are uncooperative and difficult to deal with. We just want you to be realistic in your expectations of what you can do with the time, resources, and training that is available to you. Then, there are the family, peer, and neighborhood environments to which these students return after they leave school. Chapter 11 explores the issue of dealing with difficult students.

At times, you will feel discouraged and frustrated. Some students will rebuff your efforts to connect with them. Every class will have its share of individuals who challenge you. Just remember that, like you, they are just doing the best they can with what they've got.

You may not help everyone in your classes. You probably won't make a significant difference in even the lives of most of your students. But in every class, there will be a few who will be profoundly influenced by what you do and who you are. That is what will sustain you.

10 Communicating With Parents

Silence. That was what I (Ellen) heard on the other end of the telephone. Complete stillness except for soft breathing.

I had just called a parent to say what a pleasure it was to have her child in my class, how attentive she was, and what good grades she was getting.

"Yes," she responded expectantly, "and what's your point?"

"That's all," I replied, a bit confused. Here I was telling her what a pleasure her daughter was to work with, and the mother seemed almost defensive.

"Oh," she finally said. "I was waiting for the bad news." She laughed, then said, "Are you sure?"

"Yes, I'm sure," I said, not at all sure. "I hope she continues to do well in the future."

"Well," the parent said with relief. "Thank you so much for calling! It's so nice to have a teacher call with a good report. You just made my day! I appreciate your taking the time to call."

As I hung up the phone, we both had smiles on our faces.

Calls Home

Teachers often call home when there is trouble brewing. The student is being a pest in class, or is not turning in work, or might even be failing.

The parents of many students have even become conditioned over time to associate bad news with teacher calls home. It is as if we are criticizing their parenting competence, that the kids have turned out the way they have because the parents don't know what they're doing.

Actually, we do think that, on occasion. Many of the students we see come from homes with very unhealthy living situations: Poverty and unemployment. Angry, even violent behavior among the adults. Inconsistent or little discipline. Absolutely no support for excellence in school. Hopelessness and despair. Lack of positive role models. The list goes on and on. No wonder some students struggle so much.

Still, parents are the keys to any lasting change efforts we might wish to promote. They can be our best friends or worst enemies. Without their support, they can easily sabotage any potential their children have to succeed in school or in life. Often, what we are doing is threatening to them, or at least incomprehensible. Even if their kids wanted to do their homework or prepare for class, they would be teased mercilessly by their siblings, parents, and friends. That is why it is so crucial that we connect not only with our students but also their parents.

One easy way to do that is find an excuse, almost any reason, to call parents or write them a note when their children do something that is constructive or at least a step in the right direction.

- "I've been really impressed that your daughter has come to class on time 3 days in a row. I just wanted to let you know that whatever you're doing, it seems to be working."
- "Your son turned in a paper to me this week, and although he definitely needs work with his punctuation and grammar, the ideas he expressed were really interesting. I just wanted to let you know that I think he's got some real potential."
- "I just finished grading the latest exam. Although the total score your daughter got wasn't nearly as high as I think she is capable of doing, I really liked some of her creative responses. She really has a wonderful imagination."
- "I wanted to let you know that your son really helped me out today. There was a fight that broke out in class, and he helped me regain order by acting quickly to break things up. He shows some real leadership at times. I'd love to try and build on that."

- "As you know, sometimes your daughter can be a bit challenging to keep under control. I really find her a joy to have in class, though. Her sense of humor and playfulness are lovely. I'm working with her now to be a bit more restrained at times in her comments, and I think she's making fine progress. I just wanted you to know that."

Okay, some of these are a stretch. But you get the general idea. Look for the slightest signs of improvement in your students, any evidence at all that they are growing, learning, changing, and reinforce that behavior directly by telling them how much you appreciate their efforts. Also make a point to tell their parents.

Building Parent Relationships

At the beginning of each semester, most schools now require that the teacher send home a course syllabus or class expectancy sheet. At the bottom of the page, you can have a place for the parent or guardian to sign, indicating that he or she has read the paper and is aware of the objectives, grading policy, and content of the class.

The written communication does not have to stop there. You can send a more personal letter home introducing yourself to the parents at the beginning of the school year. Periodically, or on a regular basis, you can send a general note home informing the parents of class activities, upcoming field trips, events or projects, or asking for volunteer time or objects that would be useful in the classroom.

Many parents will welcome the opportunity to be involved. They will chaperon a field trip. They will bake for a special occasion if it is permitted. They will donate products and time. They just like to be informed of what is needed, when, and where. Some will be available on a regular basis; others, infrequently; but all would probably like to be informed even if they cannot be included or involved.

Many schools send out notices midway though the card-marking period to alert parents if their children are making unsatisfactory progress (sometimes called "unsats") or are failing. Parents are generally made aware of the mailing dates of these notices. Most schools have a form you can use at any time to send the information home.

As we mentioned earlier, the telephone or E-mail can also be useful tools in communicating to parents that you need their help. Although we wish that all parent contacts involved reporting good news, it is far more likely that we contact them because their child is being noncompliant or difficult.

When you are making such contacts be very sensitive and noncritical so that parents don't become threatened and uncooperative themselves. Try to stay neutral, calm, and helpful. If you are verbally attacked or it is obvious the parent isn't listening, then disengage as best you can without making matters worse. Schedule a parent conference with the principal present, or refer the parent to the counselor, dean, or assistant principal.

Basically, you are simply informing the parent of what you have observed. Provide specific examples of what has occurred. Mention a few of the student's strengths as well as weaknesses. Then, ask for the parents' help with your problem (and it really is your concern).

Open House

Most schools hold open houses to invite the parents to meet the teacher. The open house typically takes one of two formats. The most common is that the parents are given a copy of the school schedule, and each class meets for 10 minutes. During this time, the teacher introduces himself or herself, describes the content of the class, and perhaps shows an example of student work. The grading policy may be reviewed as well. Usually, there is a minute or two for general questions. There is no time given for individual attention or conversation regarding a specific student.

A private conference can be suggested for a later date. Some schools hold parent-teacher conferences at regular times throughout the year.

The second format is where teachers sit in their room, or together in one room, such as the cafeteria or the library, and the parents line up to speak to each of their children's teachers. In this scenario, teachers introduce themselves and give a brief report on the child's progress. Although more personal in nature than the first format, there is not really time to go into any problems in depth, and a private conference can be suggested for a later date.

Face-to-Face Contacts

Formal or informal parent conferences are other fruitful methods of communication. Such meetings can include a single parent or a whole group of people, including the student, his or her parents, other family members, school administrators, a counselor, and others who might be relevant. Including the student will give him or her the opportunity to express his or her own feelings on the matter. Some schools have moved to student-led conferences, where the student is responsible for planning and leading the conference.

It is important to be prepared for the conference. First, consider setting the stage. If the conference is to be held in your room, you may need to rearrange the furniture so there will be comfortable places for the parents and you to sit face to face. If you sit behind your desk, you create a symbolic barrier. Try to find a time and place where you will not be disturbed. Post a note on your door indicating a conference is in progress.

Create a folder for the conference. In it, you will want to have examples of the student's work. You can include your written descriptions of the student's behavior. Include a printout of the student's attendance record and grades.

The first impression you make is very important. Greet the parent(s) or guardian(s) as they enter the room. Introduce yourself if this is the first meeting. Be sure to make eye contact with the adults, and say hello to the student if he or she is present. As you guide the participants into the room, say something positive about the student. Let the parents look around the room. Talk about the class in general.

As you move into the conference, you can ask a general question: "What does Lisi say about the class when she is at home?" See if you can gather some information. Use your listening skills. Then, review the purpose of the conference—was it initiated by the parent? By you? Or is this a regularly scheduled conference to review progress? If the student is present, let him or her state his or her perception of the situation and his or her feelings.

Review the objectives for the class, and see if there are any problems. If so, identify strategies that might help resolve the problems. Be specific as you determine the child's responsibilities, the parents' or guardians' responsibilities, and your own role. Try to set a time line on what needs to be done, when, where, and how. The last step is to identify how progress will be evaluated and monitored.

In concluding the conference, thank the parents for coming, and invite each person to summarize his or her understanding of the conversation. Make plans for further communication with the adults, whether that is by telephone, letter, fax, E-mail, another scheduled conference, or a progress report sent by the school.

After the conference, you can take time to write down some notes (if you didn't do so during the meeting). Reflect on what transpired. Ask yourself the following questions:

- Did I give each of the participants time to share his or her views?
- Did I mention positive aspects of the student's behavior and work as well as the problem areas?
- Was I prepared with samples of the student's work and examples of behavior?
- Did I keep the focus on the student and not the school or the parent?
- Did I maintain my composure throughout the meeting, staying empathic and responsive?
- Was a specific plan developed to foster progress in the future?
- What was forgotten or neglected that I wish to deal with in the future?

Ongoing Contact

You can direct students to take home their graded or evaluated work with a note to have signed and returned as a way to make sure the parent is kept abreast of the student's progress. You need to make sure that each student returns the work with the signature. Those who don't return papers or projects need to have their parents contacted with respect to the grade or evaluation received *and* the fact that the student did not return the work as directed. (Check for validity of parent signatures, too.)

The school newsletter is another way to communicate with parents. By submitting articles that you or one of your students have written, you can let parents know what is going on in your classroom or with your club or with your team. You can also include photographs, which will make the article more attractive.

Taking pictures of the students in various activities and sending them home is a fun way to let the parents know what the children are doing and what their involvement is. Another idea would be to make a videotape and take turns sending it home with students. This would be an especially useful plan for students whose parents don't speak English.

Making "house calls" is one other option to consider. Although time consuming, and perhaps risky without supervision or proper training, informal visits to a student's home with the parents' prior approval is another way that you can show how much you care. You can gain valuable information in that setting that would be inaccessible any other way.

Dealing With Difficult Students 11

Beginning teachers are likely to be tested and challenged by students. A lot. This isn't personal; rather, it's a rite of passage. Teenagers often just check the limits of their behavior to see how far they can go, what actions will be tolerated, and which won't.

The good news is that your colleagues and administration know this, and they will give you the time you need to find your stride. You are likely to be reassured again and again by the dean, principal, and department head that this is normal behavior, and if you experience any predicaments with students you can't handle, refer them immediately for disciplinary action.

Most often, this means a student who

- Is consistently late to class
- Repeatedly does not bring in necessary supplies
- Threatens or disrespects you, publicly or privately
- Threatens or assaults another student
- Refuses to follow your instructions
- Disrupts the class with inappropriate behavior

Depending on the policies of your administration and norms of your school, any or all of these behaviors will not be tolerated. Especially with beginning teachers, you must expect (and request) support from other school personnel to help you keep your classes under control and your students' behavior within reasonable limits. It is simply not realistic for you to expect that you can handle all discipline problems yourself, even if you had the time to do so.

Avoid Direct Confrontation

Sending a student out of the classroom should be the last resort, after you've tried everything else—reasoning, reminding, cajoling, threatening, even pleading. There are consequences to taking formal disciplinary action. For one thing, it brings attention to the fact that there was a problem you couldn't handle yourself. Although you are allowed a certain latitude in this regard, you don't want to resort to sending kids out of your classroom very frequently, or it may look like you haven't established control over your classes.

In general, whenever a student appears noncompliant, uncooperative, or defiant, whatever you do, you don't want to escalate matters by making a public show of authority or force—unless it is absolutely necessary. It is far better to censure privately. Speak in a low, calm voice. Give directions firmly but avoid threats.

Do not touch students. Some children will react violently—not only will they shake off the gesture, but they may attempt to strike back.

Remember: Everyone else in the room is watching closely to see how you handle yourself. There is a show going on, and you are the main attraction. You are being tested. Your response is crucial.

Remain cool, poised, and in control of yourself. Do not become defensive. Likewise, try not to put the student in a position in which he or she loses face in front of peers. This is a tough challenge but can be accomplished if you have instilled a reasonable discipline policy in the first place.

Implementing a Discipline Policy

Most schools have a formal discipline program that you are mandated to follow. In a way, this takes the heat off you because your job is simply to enforce the rules established by the administration (and perhaps by the students themselves). You will need to give a student warnings and perhaps be required to contact the parent(s) or guardian(s), or document an attempt to do so, before a referral can be made for routine difficulties.

Usually, all disciplinary actions call for a written report. Make sure you keep the needed forms within arm's reach. Once there is some altercation, you will want to maintain fluid motion rather than be seen fumbling around. Remember again: This is a drama that is unfolding that is usually far more interesting than what you have planned for class that day. Keep in mind your audience. Don't show disgust, frustration, anger, or other negative emotions on your face. Don't let students know that you've been rattled. It is just a game, and you are playing your role.

If you must exile a student from your classroom, do so as quickly and smoothly as you can. Do not raise your voice, even if the student screams at you. Remain infuriatingly unruffled, repeating again: "You are out of control. You must leave. Now. We will talk about this at another time."

If the student refuses to comply, a very rare situation, you will need to call for reinforcements. Meanwhile, direct the rest of the students to engage in some activity so they aren't frozen in the role of audience watching the drama unfold. Instruct the class to work with partners or in groups, some activity that increases the energy and noise level and helps them to work off the vicarious stress they will have experienced watching one of their brethren appear humiliated.

In any discipline policy, you must enforce rules consistently, fairly, and dispassionately. This is not personal; it's not about you; it's about teaching the offender, and the rest of the class, about maintaining order and appropriate boundaries for the sake of everyone's safety and comfort.

Taking Action

Taking part in a fight earns an automatic referral to the dean's or principal's office in most schools. Both or all participants must be sent. Call for security, and caution the other students away from the fight for their safety. Get help; do not try to break up a fight yourself: You may get hurt. Many well-intentioned teachers, even those who are quite large and strong, have ended up quite bruised, physically and emotionally, when they have tried to break up fights on their own. In some cases, the student(s) might even turn on you.

The unruly student, the one whose parents you've talked to three times, the one you've warned three times in class, the one who steps over the line with her distractions, will have to be exiled to the office if you are to continue instruction successfully. Take time to write the referral carefully. Many people will see your description of the situation. Write legibly with attention to grammar and spelling. A copy of the form will become part of the student's discipline folder.

You will have a couple of choices to make in how to handle the situation. You can call the student to your desk, or you can walk over to him or her. Be prepared for the student to act out in some way. She may read the referral out loud. She may protest unfair treatment. She may promise to be good and stop talking. Hold your ground. It will be over in a minute. The noise will subside, and you will be able to resume the activities you planned for the period.

If you are suspicious about whether the student will show up at the office, send an escort along. If the student refuses to go, call for help. Schools have students log in their arrival times to keep track of them. Follow up at the end of the day to see that the student did sign the log and what consequences were implemented by the dean or principal. This will allow you to check to see if other teachers have been having trouble with the same student as well. If that is the case, you may wish to consult with colleagues to coordinate some future action to prevent other problems.

After the altercation itself, you may wish to discuss the matter with the class, if that is appropriate and there is some lesson to be learned. You do not owe the students an explanation, but sometimes, it is helpful for morale to talk about conflict, resolution, and feelings. They have been witness to a "power play." Younger students may need help interpreting the situation, analyzing options, understanding authority. They may need a brief respite themselves before they are able to turn their attention to their work.

In unusual situations in which you feel emotionally overwhelmed or injured, ask for relief. An administrator, a teacher with a free period, or an aide from another room can come in for a few minutes to give you a respite, time to collect your thoughts and feelings and figure out how to approach the students.

Processing the Experience

Conflicts are opportunity for growth. They teach you about your own limits. They underscore issues of power and control. They bring to your attention unresolved issues that you may need to examine more closely. They regulate distance in relationships when one or more parties may feel threatened by intimacy. The important thing is to reflect on what happened during the altercation, what the conflict or disagreement or acting out was really about. Consider the following possibilities:

- The student was after attention and was willing to win it at any cost.
- A power struggle ensued because each of you was determined to win control.
- The student felt disrespected and felt the need to assert himself or herself.
- The student was simply being irresponsible and acting inappropriately, asking for some intervention.
- The student was manipulative, controlling, and game playing, enjoying the challenge of getting underneath your skin.
- Things escalated out of control because the student was asking for direction, structure, or limits that you weren't able or willing to provide
- You triggered the problem by asking the student to do something that he or she was unable to do.
- One of your buttons got pushed, and you overreacted.
- The student displaced anger toward you that was really directed elsewhere (a parent or other authority figure).
- You misinterpreted the situation, and the person you disciplined wasn't the primary culprit.

These are just a few of the possibilities. Usually, the situation is so complex that a number of factors are operating, some of which involve the student, some of which involve others in the class or in the student's life, and some that involve you and your own personal issues related to power and control. Most often, there is some interactive effect operating in which each of the participants in the struggle had some role in its genesis and maintenance.

For you to learn from the experience, you must reflect on what happened, what you did that may have exacerbated the problem, what you could have done differently, and what parts had nothing to do with you whatsoever. This is a very difficult task to undertake alone. It is far better to consult with a colleague to help you unravel the predicament.

A good place to begin in your learning process is to check with the dean or assistant principal who handled the matter. Get some background information about the context for the problem, if such information is relevant. Most important, arrange some time in which you can meet with the student or parents (or both) to debrief the episode and smooth things over for the future. You do not want to be stuck with an enemy in your class who is committed to revenge and payback for some perceived injustice.

Unfortunately, with some kids, there is little you can do to put things behind you. He or she enjoys the power that comes from remaining obstinate and disruptive, from challenging authority figures; the acting out becomes intrinsically rewarding no matter what you do. With some cases, you will just have to accept the limits of what is within your control. It does take two committed parties to heal a rift. Whatever happens, you must let go of things and move on. Almost every week, if not every day, there will be some similar episode. You must develop your own ways to metabolize these struggles, to not take them personally; they simply come with the job. No sense in complaining about them too much (as some teachers do constantly); that doesn't change things either and will only make you embittered. Accept the reality that in almost any class you teach, there will be a few individuals who are singularly unpleasant. This is really no different than anywhere else in the world where obnoxious, disruptive, self-centered people thrive on their ability to make others' lives as difficult as they can.

Welcoming the Student Back

Whether there has been some private conference with the offending student or not, there will be a critical time when he or she returns to your class. This could occur the next day, in a few days, or even the following semester.

You will want to avoid future repetitions of the same problem. At the same time, you want to reconnect with the student in such a way that you both can forgive, forget, and move forward. It is truly amazing, sometimes, how your best relationships with kids will evolve from these conflicts.

I (Jeffrey) worked with one student who was my worst nightmare. He was a smart-ass. He was always questioning things. He couldn't seem to sit still for long, always in motion. If truth be told, he was like me.

Initially, I tried to bring him under control, to no avail. I tried everything I could think of to stop him from being disruptive in class. Nothing worked. I consulted with many colleagues to get advice, but perhaps this young man had his own confidantes as well: Every time I came in with some new discipline strategy, he would change his own approach. He always seemed to be a step ahead of me.

We butted heads throughout the year. I spent an embarrassing amount of time thinking about him, feeling inept and incompetent. It felt like he saw through me, that he knew I was a fraud, that I didn't really know what I was doing. Actually, a part of me secretly admired him.

In time, I came to really value this boy's contributions to my class. He remained slippery and unpredictable, at times even incorrigible. I never did develop any consistent discipline plan to bring him under control. But over time, that didn't seem to matter much. We eventually developed a deep respect for one another, to the point where he actually became my favorite student. The turning point for me was confronting my own need to beat him in this battle of wills.

When the student does return to your class, try to make sure the reentry is comfortable. Let the student know if the seats in the classroom have been changed. Inform the student about what topic is being covered. Be attentive without being solicitous. Try to structure things in such a way that you can avoid future confrontations.

Respect

I (Cary) think teachers should find a balance in the ways they discipline. The best way to keep students from acting out is to make them respect you by setting specific expectations. If I respect my teacher a lot, then I'm not going to create many problems.

One teacher was just too nice. She made threats, but she never carried them out. She didn't do what she said she would. Over and over, students would do crazy things and she was powerless to stop anyone. Everyone took her as a joke. Nobody really learned much in that class. We liked the teacher, but we didn't respect her.

Respect is a two-way street. The teacher must also take into consideration the feelings and needs of the students in the room. Teenagers react well to reasonable explanations. The language you use to speak to the students as well as your tone of voice send potent messages to the class. An initial discussion of class rules and the school discipline policy, combined with conscientious planning and thorough preparation on your part, will limit the opportunities difficult students will have to test you.

Getting Involved in Activities 12

On the one hand, you will have plenty to do just staying on top of your assigned classes. The last thing you need as a brand-new teacher is added responsibilities and commitments at school. On the other hand, some of the most enjoyable and satisfying interactions you will ever have with students take place not in the traditional classroom but in extracurricular activities settings related to school clubs and sports, competitions, career, and social organizations.

Although it would be far better for you to get involved slowly in various school activities, maybe even waiting until your second year on the job, it may very well be that an opportunity arises that is too enticing to pass up. A coach or club adviser unexpectedly quits, and you are invited to take over the group. The principal approaches you with an invitation to begin or continue a particular school organization, and it wouldn't look good for you to turn it down. Or perhaps you just have this burning desire to make a difference in kids' lives in a setting that isn't so restrictive as the traditional classroom.

Activity Adviser

The things teachers most dislike about their classroom jobs are that they are constantly called on to keep students on track, to evaluate their performances, and to keep order and discipline. Furthermore, the participants are not often volunteers; they have not really chosen to be in your classes. This is quite a different circumstance in the case of extracurricular activities in which students do choose to devote their own time to participate in the enterprise. Although some students have hidden or disguised agendas not related to true devotion to the activity, they still have a degree of motivation that prevents most discipline problems. For instance, even those students who are participating in debate or a community service organization for less than altruistic reasons—because they want to beef up their resumes, please their parents, or hang out with friends—are still volunteers.

Most schools have a wide variety of service clubs, some of them related to those in the community at large. For example, the Kiwanis organization supports Key Clubs in many areas of the country. Not only do students do many hours of community service work, but they also have an opportunity to gain valuable leadership experience.

Your role as the adviser to such a school club is to keep the students on task, provide some organizational skills, and help students with their planning. Meanwhile, you have the chance to get to know students in a more informal way. Furthermore, as a result of your efforts, you really can see a difference that you are making in people's lives—not only among the clientele you are attempting to serve but also in witnessing greater maturation on the part of the students you are mentoring.

School clubs also provide a number of social opportunities for students. For those who are not involved in organized sports or who don't have jobs after school, there is a problem for most teenagers in having too much unstructured time. Kids sit anesthetized in front of the television, or play video games, or sleep all afternoon. Even worse, drugs and alcohol are used as means to deal with boredom and stress.

The reality of contemporary life is that there just aren't many places that teenagers can go after school. They may hang out at malls or convenience stores. They roam around the streets looking for something to do. Boredom, or just plain lack of stimulation and structure, are very real problems in most kids' lives. That is where school activities can serve a really useful purpose—providing structure, doing something useful, interacting with others around a common purpose, making new friends.

As an adviser to school clubs and organizations, you get to do things with students rather than plan for them. You are not so much an authority figure as you are a wise, older sibling who helps them solve their own problems.

The activities of clubs and activities are shared learning experiences based on common interests. Often, the teacher and students do things together for the first time—going on a field trip, for example. Common bonds are built, where you will hear "Remember when we . . ." Students have the opportunity to observe you in a new way and see your reactions to novel situations.

Another advantage of sponsoring a club is that you get to meet students who are not in your classes. You get to know more people, and this will help you feel more comfortable in the school. You will become aware of the social patterns in the school. You will see who are friends with whom. You will watch as attachments form among the boys and girls. You will see how new students are drawn into various groups.

Class Sponsor

Being a class sponsor is another way to get involved with students. This is certainly a big responsibility at the beginning of the school year. Most schools have homecoming traditions to maintain, including classes making floats for the homecoming parade. Again, it's another chance to get to know the students and work with them outside the classroom.

Regardless of the activity, you will have opportunities to talk to students in an informal situation, and you will increase your rapport with them.

Coaching Athletics

Although coaching a sport leads to evaluations of performance, like the classroom, it still provides another venue for teacher-student interaction. Students are intensely motivated to make the team. They know their ability will be assessed and are willing to be scrutinized.

Intense relationships develop because of the time, energy, and concentration devoted. Coaches' words are revered. Students rely on your guidance, your decisions. They know coaches look out for their welfare—making sure they maintain good grades and develop good health habits as they begin connecting with college and university scouts. You share your expertise. Students see you in a different light, making on-the-spot decisions. Students are willing to hear criticism if it will lead to improvement.

Coaches get to see the players grow and develop as they mature into young men and women. In such roles, you foster camaraderie, good work ethic, and team spirit. You teach physical and social skills, build self-esteem and confidence, create an esprit de corps in which cooperation is valued over individual accomplishment. You teach the value of practice and self-discipline. You help students overcome injury, errors, and defeat. You help kids develop class and dignity, whether they win or lose. You see bonds develop that will last the rest of their lives.

I (Cary) know that the one thing I will always remember about my high school years is playing baseball.

My coach runs my life. I'm with him more than I am with my own father. Sometimes, I am forced to run until I puke. I lift weights until I can no longer feel my arms. I have never worked so hard at anything in my life, and I can't imagine there will ever be a time that I will work harder. Even if I wanted to get into trouble, there isn't any time to do so. I leave for school at 6:30 in the morning, and I don't get home until 6:00. Even my weekends are filled with practices. And we're talking 11 months per year.

The lessons my coach teaches us aren't just about baseball but about life. It's about working together toward achieving one goal. Every day, 3 or 4 hours of practice. Sometimes, even 5 or 6 hours, in the intense heat or the bitter cold.

My coach "scares the crap out of me" sometimes, but I respect him as much as I've respected any man. He has played a large part in making me who I am. All of my time that he takes up every day is his time, too. He has devoted his whole life to helping kids like me. He receives very little extra pay and not nearly enough recognition.

Honoring School Traditions

Even if you don't have the time and inclination to actually sponsor a club or coach an athletic team, you can still become involved in after-school activities by attending and promoting important events, such as school dances, athletic contests, and school performances.

Every school has its own customs. Some schools have spirit day every Friday. Typically, the first round of activities comes during the homecoming season, with a "spirit week" organized around a theme. Each class and many clubs build floats for the homecoming parade before the game. Each day of the week has a special designation for dress. Samples might include college day—wear your favorite college T-shirt or sweatshirt, hat day—wear the cap or hat of your favorite sports team, stripe day, plaid day, '60s day, Disney character clothing day, and so forth. Although they won't often admit it, students do appreciate it when teachers get into the spirit of things.

School dances on both the middle or junior high school and high school level attract a lot of student attention. As invitations go out, some hearts will rise, others will fall. Sometimes, the invitations will be quite creative—a balloon with a message inside; a box with Hershey's kisses, only one of which has a message; a poster that you will be asked to deliver to a student in a class. The answers will be just as clever—a bottle of jelly beans with a note that says "odd means yes, even means no."

Each dance may have its own customs as well. In one district, at GR (girls' reverse, where the girls invite the boys), the couple wear matching shirts for the evening. Often, there will be a photographer to take pictures of couples and groups of friends. Then, about 2 weeks later, the pictures will arrive at school, and much student attention will be paid to the pictures—how they came out and who gets copies.

October's great event is Halloween. Will you be in costume? Schools have different policies on this, some allow modest outfits if they are not considered distracting.

November is marked by food drives around Thanksgiving. Blankets and other needed items may also be collected. Some schools collect toiletries to distribute to the homeless. Football play-offs take place in this month. Rivalries may be bitter. Also, National Education Week is celebrated the third week in November.

December may feature a toy drive for unfortunate students. There will likely be orchestra and band concerts. There will also be school assemblies.

January is the end of the semester. Most schools do not hold any activities during finals week. Many schools have a Martin Luther King Jr. Day recognition.

February is the time of the basketball play-offs. Another assembly may be held to honor winter sports. March is the beginning of spring sports.

April is often the time for another spirit week. Sometimes, seniors are honored. More dress-up days will be planned, along with an assembly and after-school activities. Participants in spring sports may be acknowledged.

At the high school level, school rings continue to be popular. Students buy them as early as their sophomore year. Many schools have special ring day celebrations when they are delivered.

The arrival of yearbooks continues to be an exciting day at any level. Many schools have a signing party—which is just like it sounds. The students receive their books and then take turns autographing them. This is a fun event to watch and participate in.

The senior year is marked by many rituals—the last homecoming, ordering graduation announcements, being measured for caps and gowns, the last game for the senior athletes, senior pictures, awards night, and of course, the senior prom. Students identify themselves by the years they graduate from high school. These are the tassels that go on the rearview mirrors of their cars or trucks. They may also write their graduation year on the windows of their cars and trucks with shoe polish.

Other Traditions

There can be some negative traditions as well. Incoming freshmen can be the target of jokes and hazing. They are frequently told to use an elevator to get to the second story of a building when there is no elevator. Do be on the lookout for lost freshmen.

There are many alumni traditions as well. Alumni return on career day to share information about their professions. Congressmen return to speak to assemblies. The high school graduates return for the homecoming game. Alumni members of the band may play a song. Alumni cheerleaders will join in the acrobatics for the playing of the school fight song. At one school, the former graduates spend the day attending an assembly in the morning, then an alumni luncheon, and last, the game in the evening. Alumni reunions are held every 10 years, if not every 5. When the school vies for a state championship, the alumni will turn out in droves, in their letter sweaters or jackets (depending on their age).

All of these events and traditions may sound a bit confusing, if not overwhelming. Over time, you will decide on what activities you wish to become involved with—as a sponsor, an adviser, a participant, or a spectator. The point is that you fully join the school culture, becoming part of the family, once you devote yourself to some extracurricular activities. Students and administration will appreciate your visible support. And you will find that spending time with students away from your classroom is a wonderful break from usual routines.

13 Networking With Professionals

S taying connected with students is certainly related to success in your job. Just as important, however, is networking with others in your school and the community. You are actually part of a team that delivers coordinated services to students. Because you can't be expected to know and do it all, you can rely on other professionals. It is important to know what resources are available and how to access them.

Support System

Teachers are members of a helping profession along with others who are part of the school team: counselors, psychologists, special-education experts, nurses, librarians, media consultants, and a host of others who keep the school running. Your fellow teachers will guide you through forms that have to be completed, field trip permission procedures, fire drills, and acquiring classroom supplies. They will also help you get to know the resources in the community, which is especially important if you have just relocated. They will become a support system for you.

Jamie was an older girl in a mixed-age Spanish 1 class who grimly made her way to her seat each day. She knew a few words in the language but was not progressing well. She looked disheveled and tired, with gray splotches under her eyes. She seemed to try and concentrate but never participated in discussions.

After several brief conversations with her, I (Ellen) learned that she worked a steady job in a local restaurant. Not too long ago, this student had been severely burned while taking pizzas out of the oven. In addition, she had just found out she was pregnant. Furthermore, she had no health insurance and no support from her family. No wonder she had little motivation to learn Spanish!

I realized that there was only so much that I could do for this young woman. The first thing I did was refer her to the school nurse, after having briefed her on the situation and some specific areas I thought might be helpful—looking at her wounds, explaining the implications of her pregnancy, referring her to the health department for medical care.

I also got her school counselor and the social worker involved, because this child had quite a number of problems related to her family, her boyfriend, and important decisions related to her pregnancy and future plans. As much as the girl seemed to trust me, I knew that I didn't have the time or the proper training to handle this all on my own. I needed help, and I was glad that it was available to relieve my burden. I don't just mean the workload—but the emotional stress of caring so much about kids like this girl and feeling like there is so little that I can do on my own.

Consultations

There are a number of situations that arise that require you to take certain actions automatically. If you suspect physical or sexual abuse with one of your students, for example, you must report such observations immediately. If you believe a student is in danger of hurting himself or herself, or someone else, you must take immediate action as well.

For various health emergencies—a student fainting or having a seizure—you must contact the health office or the principal. If the situation is one of risk, emergency medical service people will be called. There will be a number of times in which your students will have injuries in physical education that might not show up until your class, or they may have asthma attacks. In each of these cases, you must take appropriate steps to make sure the student receives proper medical care. Most schools provide teachers with a list of students who have medical problems so they can be monitored. The information will also tell what to do and whom to contact.

For various behavior problems you can't deal with on your own, there are a number of people you can consult—first of all, the parents of the offending child. Use them as consultants just as you would any other professional available.

Talk to your department chair or a more experienced teacher who is willing to mentor you. They may be able to provide some insight if they have had the student in the past or someone like him or her. Another source of help would be the guidance counselor. The counselor can call in a student to talk about behavior without any negative repercussions (i.e., the student isn't "in trouble"). A counselor can talk to students in private. Also, you can ask the counselor to come to the classroom and do a general program, for everyone, on communication skills, self-esteem, cooperation, or decision-making skills. If a student comes to you to talk about a problem that makes you uncomfortable—drugs, birth control, pregnancy—or you sense a problem situation, such as abuse or neglect, then conferring with the counselor will help you to make a referral for the student to see the counselor directly. As a transition, the three of you might talk together.

One other function counselors serve is as consultants for teachers. Feel free to talk to a counselor you trust about some of your own doubts and concerns or as a way to deal with your own stress. As an ex-counselor and current counselor educator, let me (Jeffrey) reassure you that one of the best parts of our job is working with teachers directly. I really appreciated it when teachers came to me for advice or support. After working with kids all day, especially those that get referred to our office, it is an absolute pleasure to work with motivated adults.

Likewise, you can ask a dean or an assistant principal to intervene on your behalf and talk to a student, without initiating a formal grievance procedure. In addition to the advantage of an outside party acting as a mediator in a conflict, he or she also has the advantage of a private office.

Do Your Research

Talk to other teachers as much as you can. Find out how a problem child behaves in other classes. If you work as part of a team, perhaps someone else can speak to the child on your behalf. This will send a message to the student that everyone is aware of his or her behavior, that everyone is paying attention to him or her—that expectations are for improvement.

If you are not part of a team, look up the child's schedule in the attendance office or the counselor's office and talk to other teachers. See if they have strategies that are effective that you could try. Any new measure you attempt will take some time to effect a change. Don't expect an overnight miracle, but do look for small differences in behavior.

Even if you don't refer the child to individual counseling, you can make a recommendation for placement in a support group. Most schools have ongoing groups with common themes—children of divorce, self-esteem, stress management, study skills, assertiveness training, and the like. Sometimes, these groups are run after school; more likely, the student would be pulled out of class once a week.

If there are truly serious problems with behavior, then it is likely that a referral will need to be made to someone in the community—a physician for medication review, a psychologist for regular therapy, or some other specialist who can deliver the kind of intensive, individualized service that may be required. It isn't your job to make these direct referrals on your own, but it is a good idea to know what options and services are available, should the need arise.

If you feel a student has serious academic or emotional problems, there will be a referral procedure for you to follow. There will be forms to fill out that require observation and examples of the student's behavior and work. The next step may be referral to a screening committee made up of personnel at the school. There will be a meeting with the student's parent(s) or guardian(s) for explanation and to acquire permission for testing. It may take some time before the testing can be scheduled, and then, the results will have to be evaluated. Further meetings will be held with the parent(s) or guardian(s). If, at this point, it is discovered that the student does have a special need, then an individual education plan (IEP) will be written by the special-education teacher assigned. Someone will be assigned to work with you and the student.

Information will be provided to you and appropriate resources made known to help any child with special needs. The IEP will be written taking into account the abilities of the student. Accommodations will be made for the student in your classroom. With the guidelines for mainstreaming and including children with problems in today's class-rooms, the child will probably not be removed. Rather, you will make adjustments in expectations, and extra help will be made available to the student. For help, the student may have the opportunity to go to a resource room during your class period, or the resource teacher will be able to come to your room to help—both instances require good commu-nication between the classroom teacher and the resource teacher.

Consultants are also available to you in the areas of technology and multicultural education, to name a few. A computer specialist, for example, will most likely be able to help you with your software programs or dealing with any problems that arise. They may even provide you with targeted training in areas in need of upgrade.

Another valuable person is the learning strategist. The function of this person is to provide support and help teachers develop the resources needed to teach a particular concept. They may demonstrate a lesson or present methods and materials to the classroom teacher. They may help the teacher evaluate learning styles. The strategist may come from one of many backgrounds, such as literacy or technology.

The school librarian will be a great resource for you as well. Not only does he or she know the interests and ability levels of the students, but he or she will be able to match materials to their needs. In addition, the relationships with students will be very different from yours. Librarians maintain contact with the students through 3 or 4 years and can get to know them very well. Frequently, the librarian is also responsible for the audiovisual materials, including videotapes and laser discs. He or she will be able to make recommendations to you, depending on what you are looking for.

Team Teaching

If you are not already assigned to a team, consider organizing one yourself. There are many wonderful interdisciplinary projects that can challenge your students if you coordinate your lessons with people in other fields. From studying earthquakes, to the Middle Ages, math, science, English and reading, and social studies, teachers can work together to coordinate their efforts. Set times for planning together. Coordinate your time schedule for student tests and projects. Divide the evaluation chores evenly so no one feels overburdened. Keep the communication lines open. Even if you just work with another teacher in your field, you can combine your efforts and learn from one another.

For academic richness and diversity, recruit people in the community as team members. Retired persons, for example, are often hungry for opportunities to share their lifelong expertise. Bring in guest speakers, demonstrations, performances. Professional organizations and businesses usually have lists of speakers and presentations for school children. Media people may be willing to visit your classroom to talk about relevant issues. Draw on experts and resources from the local universities. Most of all, bring in parents as helpers.

The important thing is that you are not alone. There are a number of formal channels in place that can provide you with support and networking to do your job and deal with any challenges that arise. Informal networking, as well, is invaluable, not only to help you deal with immediate problems but also to continue your own growth and education as a professional.

14 Using a Substitute

"Are you a sub?"
"What are we going to do today?"
"Do we have to sit in our seats?"
"Are we going to have the test tomorrow?"
"Where is our teacher?"
"When is our teacher going to be back?"

Just so you know, any time I (Cary) walk into class and see a substitute sitting by your desk, I rub my hands together and think to myself, "It's time to play." Having a sub means we're probably not going to be doing any work. Unless you include picture identification cards, students are going to trade names and seats. They will try to bend any rule they can. It's open season.

Try to avoid having the sub teach anything because they usually have no idea what they are talking about. Just give an assignment for the kids to work on and turn in at the end of the period. Other than that, just hope that things don't get too far out of control.

Of Necessity

There will come a time when you will need to be absent from school. You may be sick, or have a doctor's appointment, or be attending a conference, or taking a personal day for one reason or another. In any event, when you are not going to be in class, arrangements will have to be made for a substitute. The secret is to be prepared.

The procedures for arranging a substitute vary from one district to another. In one place, you may contact the substitute yourself; in another, you will contact a secretary who makes the call; in yet a third, you may telephone information to a Touch-Tone system. Usually, you will have the opportunity to state a preference for a particular person. In most systems, there will be individuals who are well acquainted with the staff, policies, and students of the school. They will be well known by the students. As a new teacher, it would be beneficial to make a point to meet these people. One opportunity to do this is in the morning, in the secretary or office manager's office, when substitutes check in. You can find out a little about their backgrounds and their experiences. Another chance to talk to substitutes will be when you see them in your hallway or in the classroom next door. You may also come into contact with them at breaks or lunchtimes. Make it a point to welcome them; you know what it feels like to be a newcomer.

Other teachers may make recommendations for you. There may be times when you have to call on someone you don't know. Whether or not you have met the substitute ahead of time, there are several things you can do to facilitate a smooth transition.

Providing Information

In preparation for an absence, whether it is anticipated or not, it is helpful to gather information together for the substitute. A suggested format can be found at the end of this chapter. In one school district in South Carolina, the high school required information be kept in a folder in the teacher's mailbox at all times. Whether you are provided with a folder or make up your own, the following points will be beneficial for anyone who takes over your classroom.

First, the substitute will need to know the correct spelling of your name, your room number(s), and the bell schedule. If your school has standard assembly schedules, a copy of these should be included, too. Although the substitute may receive a copy of the school map on arrival, it would be nice to include a map of the school with your room(s) clearly indicated, along with the nearest fire alarm, exit, bathroom, and principal's or dean's office, and teachers' lounge.

For each hour, general information about your classes will be helpful: title, description of the course, textbook(s). The substitute will need rosters of your students. You will need to update this list periodically to include additions and deletions. Likewise, include an up-to-date seating chart. Many teachers will leave a list of names of students who can advise a substitute as to class procedures. It is a good idea to leave several names for each period in case of student absences. Specific information on the lesson plan can follow. If you know in advance you will be absent, you can also include a list of students who are scheduled to be absent due to field trips or activity participation in school.

You may decide to prepare an all-purpose lesson that can be used at any time during the year. This will relieve any anxiety that you may feel when it becomes apparent that you will not be able to attend school as planned. Place the substitute plans in an area that is obvious, such as on your desk, in the top drawer of your desk, or on the file cabinet or book shelf close to your desk. Write a reference to their location in your substitute folder as well. It would be a good idea to let your neighbor teachers and your department chair know where these plans will be, as well, because these are the people the substitute will turn to for help if he or she cannot find them. Once this plan is used, you will need to create another one.

Class procedures need to be carefully described. You may have special activities that are performed each day, such as a current events discussion, a geography question, a thought for the day, or making a journal entry. Perhaps you follow a special dismissal policy. Anything you would like to see continue in your absence will have to be specified for the substitute.

Substitutes will also need information related to specific students. In this category, you will need to list students with specific medical problems and the courses of action to follow. Disabilities would be noted. You would acknowledge students who need to leave early or are permitted to arrive late. Any student who is an aide would be listed.

Special duties you have will need to be highlighted. For example, if you are responsible for hall duty at a particular place and time, this would be indicated. Let the substitute know if you have a university practicum teacher or a student teacher. The substitute will be the responsible teacher in these situations, not the practicum or student teacher (his or her responsibilities are usually limited to when the classroom teacher of record is present). Their roles need to be clarified for all parties involved.

Leave any supplies that will be needed in a conspicuous place or note where they can be found. If audiovisual equipment is needed, reference this as well—where and how to obtain the equipment. Because students complain they don't have pencil or paper to do an assignment, it will make the substitute's life easier if you leave a small reserve supply. Also, to make sure the students use the class time as intended, develop an assignment that is due at the end of the period. This does not have to be a formal project or writing assignment, it can be a brainstorming of ideas, a three-sentence summary, a picture, whatever you decide. If possible, develop something that is reasonably fun so that students will not create unnecessary discipline problems.

The substitute will need access to your school forms. The attendance will have to be reported. He or she may need to write a pass for a student. On occasion, he or she will have to write a discipline referral. Also, it is a good idea to leave paper on which the substitute can report on the students' behavior as well as how and to what extent your plan was followed. Sometimes, a specific form will be submitted to the office.

Students will want to know why you are absent and how long you will be away. If you are comfortable providing this information to the substitute and letting him or her disclose it, you will prevent a barrage of questions and help reduce the anxiety level of the classroom. Furthermore, if your absence will constitute a change in their schedule, such as a new test date, presentation schedule, or project deadline, an announcement in this regard would be beneficial as well. The more the students' welfare in considered, the smoother will be the transitions of your absence and your return.

Lesson Plans

With respect to writing a lesson plan, keep the educational flow going as much as possible. Create a meaningful experience for the students. Structure activities that are consistent with the unit of study. Write objectives that the substitute can communicate to the students so that they will know what the goals are for the period. The students need to be informed as to what will be expected of them and what they need to do to stay on task. This communication will make the best use of time for students and the substitute. Try to create a plan that will involve the substitute as a resource person.

Encourage the substitute to introduce him or herself to the class. It is important that the students get to know the alternate who is responsible for them for the day. In some ways, having a guest teacher can energize the classroom in ways that wouldn't otherwise be possible. Much depends on the quality of the professional you select for the temporary assignment and how well you have prepared that person to do the job. Following are sample forms for providing information for a substitute (Form 14.1) and for a substitute's report back to you (Form 14.2).

FORM 14.1
Information for Substitute Teacher

Teacher's Name _____ Room(s)_____

Schedule:

Period	Class	Textbook	Time	Room

Special duties
_____

Student roster: attached or in folder

Seating chart: attached or in folder

Nearest fire alarm
_____

Signal for fire alarm
_____

Nearest exit for fire alarm drill _____

Other emergency procedures: _____
_____
_____

Students with special needs:

Name	Period	Need

(continued)

FORM 14.1
Information for Substitute Teacher *(continued)*

Student helpers:

Period   Name

_____   _____

_____   _____

_____   _____

_____   _____

_____   _____

_____   _____

_____   _____

_____   _____

Helpful teachers: _____   Room _____

_____   Room _____

Location of lesson plans: _____

Location of supplies: _____

Include: __ Map
           __ Assembly schedule
           __ Excused absence list for field trip or activity participation
           __ Hall passes
           __ Discipline referral forms

FORM 14.2
Substitute Teacher Report Form

Class_____

Student Absences _____

_____

_____

Student Tardies _____

_____

_____

Lesson Plan Report _____

_____

_____

_____

Student Behavior _____

_____

_____

_____

Comments and Suggestions _____

_____

_____

_____

15 Taking Care of Yourself to Minimize Stress

O ne of the most difficult aspects of your first year as a teacher is feeling so vulnerable in your probationary position. It is not unduly paranoid of you to feel like everyone is watching you, critically evaluating your performance. If fact, your students, colleagues, and the administration are watching closely to see if you have the right stuff to make it in this profession.

Being Evaluated

As a student teacher or beginning teacher, your work in the classroom will be evaluated many, many times. Many districts have a policy in which you are observed up to a dozen different times during the first year, perhaps three of which will be written up as formal assessments of your performance.

Initially, this is an unnerving experience knowing there is someone in your room who is watching every move you make, forming impressions on your competence and worthiness as a teacher. Much of this stress can be alleviated if you prepare yourself ahead of time, rehearsing the things you will do and say once you are subjected to scrutiny. Of course, sometimes, you simply won't be able to control what happens in your class on any given day. Administrators realize this, of course, which is why they return so many times to give you the benefit of the doubt on those days when you are not functioning at your full potential.

Some things are within your control, regardless of how the students act or how well-received a particular unit goes. Keep an upbeat attitude. Work from a position of strength. Be prepared. Keep your lesson plans up to date. Return papers in a timely way. Average grades frequently. Always have an alternative idea in mind in case your timing is off—a lesson is completed sooner than you anticipated or students fail to comprehend an important point and are not ready to move on to the next step.

It's perfectly natural to feel nervous when an administrator enters the room. My secret (Ellen) is to take a deep breath, welcome the person, help him or her find a place to sit (sometimes, not an easy task). Then, I provide the visitor with a copy of the book or resource materials I am using. Sometimes, I give the observer my copy and I share with a student. This gives me time to gain my composure. Then, I continue with my plan.

Some administrators will visit for an entire period. Others will check in on your class at the beginning, the middle, the end—and not necessarily in that order. Do not worry that they have missed your opening activity if they walk in during the middle of a session. They may ask you about it at a later time, or perhaps they are looking at another area of your teaching. Most of them have experience, and if you are acting in a competent manner, they do not necessarily stay very long.

Let your administrators know what is going on in your classes informally as well. These days, most administrators have hall duty or lunch duty. Find out where their assignments are and visit with them from time to time. Invite them to see your room or to stop by at a particular time when you have something special planned that would be of interest.

Things to Expect

As in most things in life, you can reduce stress considerably if you know what to expect. Familiarize yourself with the evaluation forms that are used by your administration. Ask to see samples (with names deleted) of evaluations that are particularly glowing as well as those that are deficient. Before you are subjected to formal evaluation by an administrator, ask an experienced colleague to visit your class and give you preliminary feedback. This can act as a dress rehearsal for the real thing, and you can get used to being observed while you work.

The beginning of the school year is a very busy time for everyone. Most administrators do not observe during the first couple of weeks. They will give you time to get to know your students, institute your policies, and set up your routines. If you are not informed by the teacher's manual or during your orientation when the evaluation deadlines are, you can ask the other teachers. They will notice when the administrators are walking around the building with their notebooks. You can anticipate a visit soon thereafter.

Some districts have formal observations where you will be informed of a visit ahead of time. If you have a test scheduled for that time, let the administrator know. You need to be observed in action, demonstrating your energy, your skill, your content knowledge base, your rapport with the students. Some kinds of presentations lend themselves to a more accurate display of what you can do.

Warn your students of what may happen so they don't overreact to the visit. Under the best of circumstances, they will cooperate in such a way as to show you at your best.

The review of the observation will generally take place a day or more later. Most supervisors will write a narrative description of the behavior as well as complete a checklist. Districts often include "directions for the future," no matter how good you are, so don't be put off by a list of "charges." It may be a recommendation to continue an approach or to monitor a behavior or to get involved in extracurricular activities. As a novice, expect a critical review. Some administrators believe they aren't doing their jobs properly if they can't find fault with some things you do, no matter how nitpicky. Use the comments constructively.

Most evaluation forms require that you sign them, indicating you have read what is included. You are given an opportunity to respond if you like, but be careful that you aren't perceived as defensive or unwilling to accept feedback. Try to be gracious and grateful for whatever the administrators have offered.

Other Sources of Stress

Although being evaluated is one source of stress in your life, it is hardly the only one. Teaching is a physically and mentally demanding profession. You are constantly on your feet, under the gun, making quick decisions, responding to one situation after another. Mistakes and misjudgments are inevitable. You will need to be forgiving with yourself and your limitations; after all, you are a beginner.

In addition to the self-inflicted stress caused by your own unrealistic expectations and fears of failure, there are also those related to the profession itself. You are overworked and underpaid. You have far too many students in your classes and far too much work to complete within the time available.

The politics in your school can eat you alive. Common to any human organization, gossip can be treacherous. Backbiting, infighting, and coalitional battles are routine. Administrators are somewhat less supportive than most people would prefer. They have their own pressures to face with limited budgets and resources.

Some students will be a source of stress in your life. They will haunt you at night, invade your dreams, as well as preoccupy your waking moments. At times, you will feel helpless and frustrated, wondering why some students treat you so poorly and are so unappreciative of your best efforts to help them. Some parents, as well, will attempt to make your life miserable. They will blame you for their kids' problems, hold you responsible for every misfortune. Sometimes, they will speak to you in ways that are rude, disrespectful, and hostile. All of this takes bites out of your soul.

There is an expression among mental health experts about not allowing others to live in your head rent free. What this means is that it's hard enough putting up with abusive individuals at school. What you do with those events afterward is completely up to you. If you choose (and it is a choice) to invite difficult students, parents, colleagues, and administrators to invade your private time, then your stress levels will escalate. If, on the other hand, you accept that being around some annoying people comes with the job and you shrug it off as best you can, you are likely to metabolize struggles and conflicts much easier.

Some schools are simply not very healthy environments. With overcrowded buildings, involuntary "clients," unappreciated staff, inadequate resources, and a pressured atmosphere, a certain amount of stress is a given. When morale is low, when political fighting is high, when administrators are not sensitive to teacher issues, when students are unmotivated and underachieving, things will be even worse.

We don't mean to discourage you, merely to be realistic with you about what to expect. This will allow you to metabolize problems easier when they arise. You don't have to make it a big deal when you hear colleagues complain a lot. You don't have to become unduly upset when you observe teachers being mean or insensitive to one another. You don't have to be surprised when someone works behind the scenes to sabotage you or an angry parent unloads on you. All of this comes with the territory. It doesn't have to be a big deal unless you make it so.

Take Care of Yourself

There are number of things you can do to help yourself deal with the pressures and stress you will face every day.

Write your story. Keep a journal of your first year as a teacher. Talk to yourself on paper every day or at least several times per week. Write about the frustrations you are feeling and what you intend to do about them. Set goals for yourself. Make priorities about things you intend to change. Analyze your own behavior as well as that of those around you. Confront your whining and complaining. Force yourself to think positively about what you are doing. Be forgiving of your lapses and mistakes. Try to create some meaning to the struggles you are going through. Learn from what you are living through so you can make yourself stronger and more resourceful in the future.

Structure your days sensibly. Make an appointment with yourself to take care of paperwork. Note deadlines, identify what information you need to fill out reports. Do the preliminary preparation—such as counting tardies and absences and averaging grades first. Also, build in time every day for rest and relaxation. Exercise faithfully. Eat properly. Make sure you have some fun every day.

Prioritize. Not all requests for information must be completed and submitted immediately. Deadlines will vary. Decide which of the many tasks—reports, lesson planning, grading papers—need to be completed first. If necessary, create a list of when things are due and stick with your commitments to complete them.

Take breaks. Use the time between classes to relax, to chat with a neighbor teacher, or to greet the incoming students. Let yourself enjoy your lunch period.

Be playful. Beginning teachers can be so grim, so overserious. This is important stuff you are doing, but it isn't rocket science in which a single slip will destroy the universe. Try not to take yourself so seriously. Students, in particular, really appreciate teachers who will later loosen up a bit, play with them, try to create some fun. When you are having fun in your job, then students are more likely to enjoy their learning.

Set realistic goals for yourself. Keep your ambitions high, but realize it will take time to accomplish your goals. As a new teacher, you will need considerable preparation time. With experience, you will become more proficient at what you do and will be able to use your past experiences as a basis on which to improve in the future rather than constantly inventing new solutions as to how best to teach a lesson.

Diversify your life. Structure your lifestyle in such a way that you take time away from teaching to do other things. Hang around non-teachers. Create interests in multiple areas so when one aspect of your life isn't going as well as you like, you have others to feel fulfilled.

Nourish yourself with love. Surround yourself with others who love and care for you and who you can love in return. If you don't currently have a supportive family, a loving partner, or enough stimulating friends, look hard at yourself and what you can do to fill in these gaps. If needed, get some help for yourself.

Get enough sleep. People can forgo food much easier than they can forgo sleep. After school, go home and take a nap. Reenergize for the evening ahead.

Teach your friends and family what it means for you to be a teacher. Educate them about the stresses and strains you face every day. Keep them informed about your struggles. Invite them to become part of your teaching world, or they will be left behind.

Leave your personal problems at home. Focus on your students during the workday. If you allow yourself to become distracted and distressed by other issues in your life, you not only can't do much about them at school, but you will also shortchange your students. If you have some real problems in your life, get some help.

Seek counseling and continued growth. You don't have to have severe problems or major issues to get some help from a professional. Counseling should, in fact, be mandatory for beginning teachers because of the pressures you experience and the personal changes you undergo. There will be few times in your life when you encounter so many new things about yourself and the world. A counselor can help you make sense of what you are living through and integrate those insights in your work and life.

Planning for Your Future 16

Teaching is an ongoing activity. It is one that requires continual professional growth, that is, if you want to avoid becoming like some of the burnouts you see going through the motions in your school, counting the months until retirement. Don't kid yourself: Once upon a time, they were just like you. Filled with enthusiasm and excitement. Determined to change the world. Convinced they would be different from the older teachers they made fun of. Look at them now.

What distinguishes those teachers who remain passionately committed to their jobs versus those who have all but given up is that the former group has worked hard to keep themselves fresh and vibrant. They love what they do because they teach what they love.

If you hope to have a long, distinguished career as a teacher, not as someone who does a credible job but rather as one who strives for excellence, then the seeds for this passion must be planted now. Much depends on who you choose as your mentors, who you surround yourself with as a support system, and how hard you are willing to work on your growth and development. Just like an athlete who works out every day, practices skills religiously, studies new innovations, and keeps himself or herself in peak physical shape, you, too, must devote yourself to superb conditioning—not only of your body but your mind and your spirit as well.

In this book, we have presented constructive advice from the perspectives of a teacher, a teacher educator, and a student on what it takes not only to survive your first year in the profession but to truly flourish. This may help you get through the first year, but what happens after that?

Ironically, in some ways, your first year is the easiest one in the sense that you have no worries about keeping your excitement and enthusiasm at peak levels. Unfortunately, as some teachers gain experience, they also lose some of the spark they once had, the innocence that led them to believe anything was possible, that they really could make a difference.

Right now, you have something very, very precious: your own strong belief that you will be different. You will be the kind of teacher who keeps the momentum going, who continues to commit yourself to future growth, who is always learning, always reinventing yourself. You will be the kind of teacher who students revere and admire, not just for what you know but for who you are as a human being. Your love and compassion and empathy are transparent, for anyone to see. The kids know how much you care.

This image of the kind of teacher you wish to be can indeed be yours. Much depends on how committed you remain to following through with your intentions.

Become Who You Wish Your Students to Be

If you want your students to become fearless, constructive risk takers, show them the way by how you lead your own life. If you want them to venture into the unknown, do so yourself. If you would like them to be the kinds of people who are honest, truth seeking, and sincere, then be that yourself. More than anything you say, kids pay attention to who you are.

Travel

There is only so much that you can learn from school and books and movies. See the world or as much of it as you can. Expose yourself to different cultures. Collect stories of your adventures that make your classes come alive.

Continuing Education

Most states require continued education as part of an ongoing licensing process. You must receive a certain number of university credits or professional development education credits to recertify. Some school districts offer their own professional development courses. Others offer financial incentives after teachers receive a set number of university credits. You will learn new ideas, broaden your knowledge base, and keep abreast of the latest developments in your field.

Professional Organizations

Join teacher organizations on the local and national levels. Your content area professional organization will provide you with social contacts and educational programs. It is a way to keep up to date on what is happening in the local district as well as at state and national levels.

Reflect on Your Future

Do you see yourself staying in the same position in the same school for most of your career? Are there other positions you have in mind, such as a coach, an administrator, a counselor, or school psychologist? Will you sponsor a new club or coach a different sport? Will you turn to another area of education—curriculum development or administration? Will you share your expertise with others as presenters at conferences? Will you write articles for a professional journal? Will you teach at a local university?

Might you want to teach abroad for a period of time? If so, there are a number of opportunities for exchanges, teaching in American schools abroad and brief sojourns organized by various organizations.

Look for Change

Teachers who thrive in the profession are those who keep themselves fresh and energized. They are constantly tinkering with their methods. They make changes in the ways they operate. They seek new ways to reach children more effectively.

One way to avoid boredom, burnout, and cynicism is to look for changes you can make in what you teach, how you teach, and where you teach. You can change grade levels or specialties. You can go back to school to change the focus of your work. You can team teach with others you have recruited so you can learn about alternative strategies and styles. You can switch schools or jobs. Or harder still, you can persevere with basically the same job but make significant changes in the ways you do it.

In spite of all the specific suggestions we have made and how hungry you are for even more detailed advice, there is a bigger picture involved. Don't sweat the small stuff. Your main priority your first year of teaching is getting through it with your sanity, health, and enthusiasm intact. Without that, you won't have a second year or a third.

The best teachers you ever had were able to convince you, on a primary level, that you had something important to offer others. That is your real job, to find the best that children have to offer and help them to discover this potential for themselves.